Mastering Articulate Storyline

Build up your e-learning development skills with Articulate Storyline

Ashley Chiasson

BIRMINGHAM - MUMBAI

Mastering Articulate Storyline

First published: June 2016

Production reference: 1210616

Published by Packt Publishing Ltd.

Livery Place

35 Livery Street

Birmingham B3 2PB, UK.

ISBN 978-1-78355-091-3

www.packtpub.com

Credits

Author

Ashley Chiasson

Reviewers

Matt Guyan
Helen Tyson

Commissioning Editor

Pramila Balan

Acquisition Editor

Reshma Raman

Content Development Editor

Prashanth G Rao

Technical Editor

Murtaza Tinwala

Copy Editor

Sameen Siddiqui

Project Coordinator

Bijal Patel

Proofreader

Safis Editing

Indexer

Mariammal Chettiyar

Production Coordinator

Manu Joseph

Cover Work

Manu Joseph

About the Author

Ashley Chiasson is an instructional designer and consultant with nearly a decade of experience developing high-quality e-learning solutions for various clients. She holds a Master's in Education (post-secondary studies) and a Bachelor of Arts (linguistics and psychology). In addition to being a small business owner, Ashley works for Mount Saint Vincent University, Canada, as their resident instructional developer. As a self-proclaimed ambassador of the Articulate software, Ashley truly believes that the only thing standing between you and your ability to create engaging and interactive e-learning projects is your imagination.

With a strong belief in creating her own professional freedom, Ashley has become a successful entrepreneur, working hard to find a place for her in the big world of e-learning. She works hard to ensure that her clients are satisfied, because without them, entrepreneurship would be a lonely place.

You can follow Ashley on Twitter (`@amdchiasson`) or find out more about her through her website (`http://ashleychiasson.com`).

About the Reviewers

Matt Guyan has been working in the learning and development field since 2007, starting as a classroom facilitator and workplace assessor, then moving into instructional design (for classroom and online environments).

Matt is currently a solutions developer at B Online Learning where he delivers certified Articulate Storyline 2 training as well as the online Master eLearning course. He's also a proud Articulate Community Super Hero.

Matt's interests include eLearning, performance support, community building, and motivation. He has a keen interest in how people learn and the cognitive processing that takes place as we acquire new knowledge and skills and believes applying principles around human cognitive architecture will assist in designing better learning programs and materials, leading to superior personal and organisational outcomes. He's currently completing a Master of Education in Educational Psychology at the University of NSW.

Helen Tyson is an experienced trainer, instructional designer and e-learning developer. She has been involved in training for over 15 years, focusing specifically on e-learning since 2006. She has worked in a variety of industries, including telecommunications, e-mail order retail, financial services, and clinical software production. After using several other content development software packages, she found Articulate Studio in 2009 and has not looked back since then. This led her to take part in the very first Articulate Certified Training course held in the UK for Articulate Studio.

Currently, Helen is an instructional designer and lead trainer for Omniplex Ltd., a company that provides a comprehensive range of e-learning solutions to customers across the UK, Europe, North America, and Asia. Omniplex is the Articulate Certified Training Partner for the UK and Ireland, and a large part of Helen's role is to deliver the Articulate Certified Program for Storyline and Studio, as well as Instructional Design courses. In addition to training, she works on content development projects, course consultancy, and implements LMS portals. She has previously reviewed *Learning Articulate Storyline, Packt Publishing*, by Stephanie Harnett and *Articulate Storyline Essential, Packt Publishing* also by Ashley Chiasson.

www.PacktPub.com

eBooks, discount offers, and more

Did you know that Packt offers eBook versions of every book published, with PDF and ePub files available? You can upgrade to the eBook version at www.PacktPub.com and as a print book customer, you are entitled to a discount on the eBook copy. Get in touch with us at customercare@packtpub.com for more details.

At www.PacktPub.com, you can also read a collection of free technical articles, sign up for a range of free newsletters and receive exclusive discounts and offers on Packt books and eBooks.

https://www2.packtpub.com/books/subscription/packtlib

Do you need instant solutions to your IT questions? PacktLib is Packt's online digital book library. Here, you can search, access, and read Packt's entire library of books.

Why subscribe?

- Fully searchable across every book published by Packt
- Copy and paste, print, and bookmark content
- On demand and accessible via a web browser

Table of Contents

Preface

Articulate Storyline is an incredibly powerful e-learning authoring tool, but much of its functionality goes untapped—not for long!

As you read through this book, you'll get hands-on experience creating some pretty cool interactions that go beyond the basics of Storyline. You'll quickly find out just how easy it is to create crowd-pleasing, advanced e-learning elements that build on the basic concepts of Storyline.

Storyline is near and dear to my heart, and once you begin developing in it, I'm confident that the reasons why will become apparent. Acting as a one-stop-shop for e-learning authoring, you no longer need to work across authoring tools to create elements such as interactive video, software simulations, or high-quality audio.

This book takes you beyond the basic concepts of Storyline, allowing you to learn ways of bending the program to your will! Working through the chapters, you will be amazed with some of the things you create—not realizing how powerful Storyline is. By the time you finish this book, you'll be running to show off your e-learning talent to all of your colleagues, and you'll be the Storyline sensei of your office!

With relevant exercises, this book aims to provide you with tons of opportunities to get down and dirty with Storyline, testing out new concepts and applying Storyline features in a variety of contexts.

What this book covers

Chapter 1, *Before You Begin*, provides some best practices for development, allowing you to enhance your efficiency. You will learn methods for effectively structuring projects for optimal organization, and ways in which you may streamline your development process.

Chapter 2, *Refresher of Key Concepts*, takes you back to basics by providing an overview of key concepts.

Chapter 3, *Creating a Content-Rich Story*, explores some of the more advanced aspects of adding content to your story, such as working with properties and using each content type to its fullest potential. Some Storyline 2-specific content will be discussed as well as some helpful tips and tricks.

`Chapter` 4, *Engaging Your Learners with Interactivity*, shows you how to do some cool things to make your stories more interactive. Discussing some Storyline 2-specific functionality such as motion paths and new animation options, as well as button sets, markers, and zoom region "hacks".

`Chapter` 5, *Using Variables, Conditions, and JavaScript*, explains how you can leverage variables, conditions, and JavaScript to create some really neat interactions in Storyline. You will be provided with walkthrough-style examples and plenty of exercises. You will learn how to personalize stories and create some more advanced variable-based interactions, and then you'll learn how to use some simple JavaScript to really wow your users!

`Chapter` 6, *Assessing Learners*, focuses on convert-to-freeform question creation, programming, and troubleshooting, emphasizing the development of feedback masters.

`Chapter` 7, *Preparing to Publish Your Story*, explains how to customize the player and prepare your stories for publishing. Some sections will identify how to move past the basic look and feel of a non-customized player to create a truly unique learning experience. Various publishing options will be discussed, as well as how to troubleshoot some common publishing issues.

`Chapter` 8, *Becoming More Creative*, provides you with some ideas for harnessing your inner creative to do cool things in Storyline.

`Appendix`, *Streamlining Your Development*, focuses on how you can streamline your Storyline development by using some productivity-boosting functionality.

What you need for this book

To ensure you reach your full potential in following along with this book, it is recommended that you have the following:

- An Articulate Storyline 1 or Articulate Storyline 2 license or trial (preferably Articulate Storyline 2)
- Some creativity

Refer to Articulate's website for a full list of hardware requirements recommended for operating Articulate Storyline.

Who this book is for

This book is for anyone experienced in using the basic functions of Articulate Storyline who are yearning to learn more. It's designed to provide a brief overview of key concepts and to help you refresh your knowledge of common functions, while teaching you how to push Storyline to the limit!

Conventions

In this book, you will find a number of text styles that distinguish between different kinds of information. Here are some examples of these styles and an explanation of their meaning.

Code words in text, database table names, folder names, filenames, file extensions, pathnames, dummy URLs, user input, and Twitter handles are shown as follows: "These filenames will be managed within a spreadsheet, housed within the main `200>Media` folder."

New terms and **important words** are shown in bold. Words that you see on the screen, for example, in menus or dialog boxes, appear in the text like this: "You can also use **STORY VIEW** to plan out the movement of existing scenes."

A block of code is set as follows:

```
if (document.body){
document.body.background = "BGImage.png";
}
```

 Warnings or important notes appear in a box like this.

 Tips and tricks appear like this.

Reader feedback

Feedback from our readers is always welcome. Let us know what you think about this book—what you liked or disliked. Reader feedback is important for us as it helps us develop titles that you will really get the most out of.

To send us general feedback, simply e-mail `feedback@packtpub.com`, and mention the book's title in the subject of your message.

If there is a topic that you have expertise in and you are interested in either writing or contributing to a book, see our author guide at `www.packtpub.com/authors`.

Customer support

Now that you are the proud owner of a Packt book, we have a number of things to help you to get the most from your purchase.

Downloading the example code

You can download the example code files for this book from your account at `http://www.packtpub.com`. If you purchased this book elsewhere, you can visit `http://www.packtpub.com/support` and register to have the files e-mailed directly to you.

You can download the code files by following these steps:

1. Log in or register to our website using your e-mail address and password.
2. Hover the mouse pointer on the **SUPPORT** tab at the top.
3. Click on **Code Downloads & Errata**.
4. Enter the name of the book in the **Search** box.
5. Select the book for which you're looking to download the code files.
6. Choose from the drop-down menu where you purchased this book from.
7. Click on **Code Download**.

You can also download the code files by clicking on the **Code Files** button on the book's webpage at the Packt Publishing website. This page can be accessed by entering the book's name in the **Search** box. Please note that you need to be logged in to your Packt account.

Once the file is downloaded, please make sure that you unzip or extract the folder using the latest version of:

- WinRAR / 7-Zip for Windows
- Zipeg / iZip / UnRarX for Mac
- 7-Zip / PeaZip for Linux

The code bundle for the book is also hosted on GitHub at `https://github.com/PacktPublishing/Mastering-Articulate-Storyline`. We also have other code bundles from our rich catalog of books and videos available at `https://github.com/PacktPublishing/`. Check them out!

Downloading the color images of this book

We also provide you with a PDF file that has color images of the screenshots/diagrams used in this book. The color images will help you better understand the changes in the output. You can download this file from `https://www.packtpub.com/sites/default/files/downloads/MasteringArticulateStoryline_ColorImages.pdf`.

Errata

Although we have taken every care to ensure the accuracy of our content, mistakes do happen. If you find a mistake in one of our books—maybe a mistake in the text or the code—we would be grateful if you could report this to us. By doing so, you can save other readers from frustration and help us improve subsequent versions of this book. If you find any errata, please report them by visiting `http://www.packtpub.com/submit-errata`, selecting your book, clicking on the **Errata Submission Form** link, and entering the details of your errata. Once your errata are verified, your submission will be accepted and the errata will be uploaded to our website or added to any list of existing errata under the Errata section of that title.

To view the previously submitted errata, go to `https://www.packtpub.com/books/content/support` and enter the name of the book in the search field. The required information will appear under the **Errata** section.

Piracy

Piracy of copyrighted material on the Internet is an ongoing problem across all media. At Packt, we take the protection of our copyright and licenses very seriously. If you come across any illegal copies of our works in any form on the Internet, please provide us with the location address or website name immediately so that we can pursue a remedy.

Please contact us at `copyright@packtpub.com` with a link to the suspected pirated material.

We appreciate your help in protecting our authors and our ability to bring you valuable content.

Questions

If you have a problem with any aspect of this book, you can contact us at `questions@packtpub.com`, and we will do our best to address the problem.

1
Before You Begin

You've probably been working in Articulate Storyline for quite some time now. You may be well versed with the basic development functions. You may be looking for ways of pushing Storyline to its limits. If you can relate to any of these scenarios, this book has got your curiosities covered.

Let's learn how to leverage the full potential of Storyline. This chapter provides you with an introduction to the purpose of this book and best practices related to e-learning product development, which will be explained in greater detail in the appendix.

In this chapter, we will cover the following topics:

- Pushing Articulate Storyline to the limit
- Best practices
- How to be mindful of reusability
- Methods for organizing your project
- The differences between storyboarding and rapid development
- Ways of streamlining your development

Pushing Articulate Storyline to the limit

The purpose of this book is really to get you comfortable with pushing Articulate Storyline to its limits. Doing this may also broaden your imagination, allowing you to push your creativity to its limits.

There are so many things you can do within Storyline and a lot of those features, interactions, or functions are overlooked because they just aren't used all that often. Often times, the basic functionality overshadows the more advanced functions because they're easier, they often address the need, and they take less time to learn. That's understandable, but this book is going to open your mind to many more things that are possible when using this tool.

You'll get excited, frustrated, excited again, and probably frustrated a few more times, but, with all of the practical activities for you to follow along with (and/or reverse engineer), you'll be mastering Articulate Storyline and pushing it to its limits in no time! If you don't quite *get* one of the concepts that have been explained, don't worry. You'll always have access to this book and the activity downloads as a handy reference or refresher.

Best practices

Before you get too far into your development, it's important to take some steps to streamline your approach by establishing best practices—doing this will help you become more organized and efficient. Everyone has their own process, so this is by no means a prescribed format for the *proper* way of doing things. These are just some recommendations, from personal experience, that have proven effective as an e-learning developer. Please note that these best practices are not necessarily Storyline-related, but are best practices to consider ahead of development within any e-learning project.

Your best practices will likely be project-specific in terms of how your clients or how your organization's internal processes work. Sometimes you'll be provided with a storyboard ahead of development and sometimes you'll be expected to rapidly develop one. Sometimes you'll be provided with all the multimedia ahead of development and sometimes you'll be provided with multimedia after an alpha review. You may want to do a content dump at the beginning of your development process or you may want to work through each slide from start to finish before moving on. Through experience and observation of what other developers are doing, you will learn how to define and adapt your best practices.

When a new project comes along, it's always a good idea to employ some form of organization. There are many great reasons for this, some of which include being mindful of reusability, maintaining and organizing project and file structure, and streamlining your development process. This chapter aims to provide you with as much information as necessary to ensure that you are effectively organizing your projects for enhanced efficiency and an understanding of why these methods should always be considered *best practices*.

How to be mindful of reusability

When I think about reusability in e-learning, I think about objects and content that can be reused in a variety of contexts. Developers often run into this when working on large projects or in industries that involve trade-specific content. When working on multiple projects within one sector, you may come across assets used previously in one course (for example, a 3D model of an aircraft) that may be reused in another course with the same content base.

Being able to reuse content and/or assets can come in handy as it can save you resources in the long run. Reusing previously established assets (if permitted to do so, of course) would reduce the amount of development time various departments and/or individuals need to spend.

Best practices for reusability might include creating your own content repository and defining a file naming convention that will make it easy for you to quickly find what you're looking for. If you're extra savvy, you can create a metadata-coded database, but that might require a lot more effort than you have available.

While it does take extra time to either come up with a file naming convention or apply metadata tagging to all assets within your repository, the goal is to make your life easier in the long run. Much like the dreaded *administrative tasks* required of small business owners, it's not the most sought-after task, but it's a necessary one, especially if you truly want to optimize efficiency!

Within Articulate Storyline, you may want to maintain a repository of themes and interactions so you can use elements of these assets for future development and save yourself a lot of time. Most projects, in the early stages, require an initial prototype for the client to sign off on the general look and feel. In this prototyping phase, having a repository of themes and interactions can really make the process a lot smoother because you can call on previous work in order to easily facilitate the elemental design of a new project.

Storyline allows you to import content from many sources (for example, PowerPoint, Articulate Engage, Articulate Quizmaker, and more), so don't feel limited to just reusing Storyline interactions and/or themes. Just structure your repository in an organized manner and you will be able to easily locate the files and file types that you're looking to use at a later date.

Another great thing Articulate Storyline is good for when it comes to reusability is question banks! Most courses contain questions, knowledge checks, assessments, or whatever you want to call them, but all too seldom do people think about compiling these questions in one neat area for reuse later on. Instead, people often add new question slides, add the question, and go on their merry development way. If you're one of those people, you need to *STOP*. Your life will be entirely changed by the concept of question banks—if not entirely, at least a little bit, or at least the part of your life that dabbles in development will be changed in some small way.

Question banks allow you to create a *bank* of questions (who would have thought) and call on these questions at any time to place within your story—reusability at its finest, at least in Storyline.

Methods for organizing your project

Organizing your project is a necessary evil. Surely there is someone out there who loves this process, but for others who just want to develop all day and all night, there may be a smaller emphasis placed on organization. However, you can take some simple steps to organize your project that can be reused for future projects.

Within Storyline, the organizational emphasis of this chapter will be placed on using Story View and optimizing the use of scenes. These are two elements of Storyline that, depending on the size of your project, can make a world of difference when it comes to making sense of all the content you've authored and in terms of making the structure of your content more palatable.

Using the Story View

Story View is such a great feature of Storyline! It provides you with a bird's eye view of your project or story and essentially shows you a visual blueprint of all the scenes and slides. This is particularly helpful in projects that involve a lot of branching. Instead of seeing the individual parts, you're seeing the parts as they represent the whole—the Gestalt psychology would be proud! You can also use **Story View** to plan out the movement of existing scenes or slides if content isn't lining up quite the way you want it to:

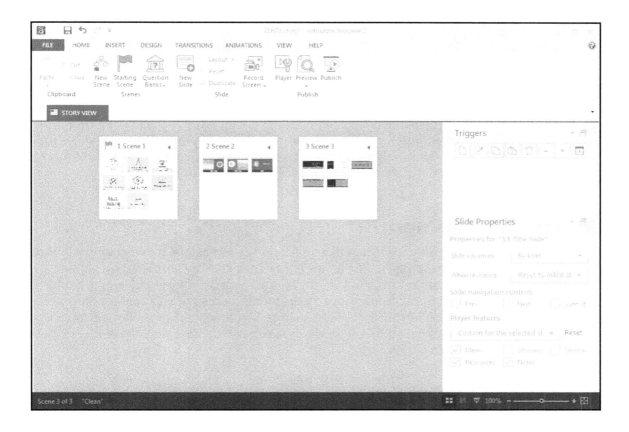

Optimizing scene use

Scenes play a very big role in maintaining organization within your story. They serve to group slides into smaller segments of the entire story and are typically defined using logical breaks. However, it's all up to you how you decide to group your slides. If the story you're working on consists of multiple topics or modules, each topic or module would logically become a new scene.

Visually, scenes work in tandem with Story View in that, while you're in Story View, you can clearly see the various scenes and move things around appropriately. Functionally, scenes serve to create submenus in the main Storyline menu, but you can change this if you don't want to see each scene delineated in the menu.

From an organization and control perspective, scenes can help you reel in unwieldy and overwhelming content. This particularly comes in handy with large courses, where you can easily lose your place when trying to track down a specific slide of a scene, for example, in a sea of 150 slides. In this sense, scenes allow you to chunk content into more manageable scenes within your story and will likely allow you to save on development and revision time.

Using scenes will also help when it comes to previewing your story. Instead of having to wait to load 150 slides each time you preview, you can choose to preview a scene and will only have to wait for the slides in that scene to load—perhaps 15 slides of the entire course instead of 150. Scenes really are a magical thing!

Asset management

Asset management is just what it sounds like—managing your assets. Now, your *assets* may come in many forms, for example, media assets (your draft and/or completed images/video/audio), customer furnished assets (files provided by the client, which could be raw images/video/audio/PowerPoint/Word documents, and so on), or content output (outputs from whichever authoring tool you're using). If you've worked on large projects, you will likely relate to how unwieldy these assets can become if you don't have a system in place for keeping everything organized.

This is where the management element comes into play.

Structuring your folders

Setting up a consistent folder structure is really important when it comes to managing your assets. Structuring your folders may seem like a daunting administrative task, but, once you determine a structure that works well for you and your projects, you can copy the structure for each project. So yeah, there is a little bit of up front effort, but the headache it will save you in the long run when it comes to tracking down assets for reuse is worth the effort! Again, this folder structure is in no way prescribed, but it is a recommendation and one that has worked well. It looks something like the following:

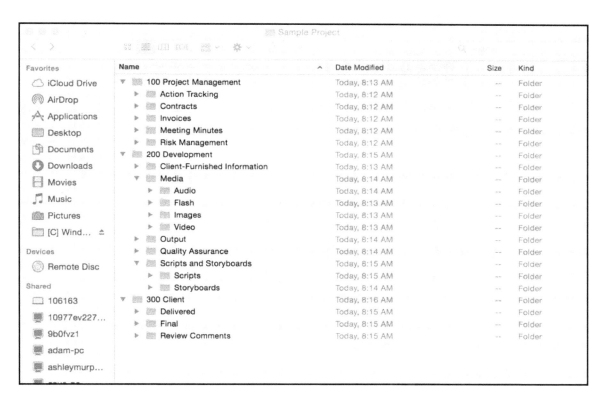

It may look overwhelming, but it's really not that bad. There are likely more elements accounted for here than you may need for your project, but all the main elements are included and you can customize it as you see fit. This is how the folder structure breaks down:

```
Project Folder:
  • 100 Project Management
    • Depending on how large the project is, this folder may have subfolders, for
      example:
      o  Meeting Minutes
      o  Action Tracking
      o  Risk Management
      o  Contracts
      o  Invoices
  • 200 Development
    • This folder typically contains subfolders related to my development, for example:
      o  Client-Furnished Information (CFI)
      o  Scripts and Storyboards
         ▪  Scripts
            •  Audio Narration
         ▪  Storyboards
         ▪  Media
            •  Video
            •  Audio
               o  Draft Audio
               o  Final Audio
            •  Images
            •  Flash
         ▪  Output
         ▪  Quality Assurance
  • 300 Client
    • This folder will include anything sent to the client for review, for example:
      o  Delivered
      o  Review Comments
      o  Final
```

Within these folders, there may be other sub-folders, but this is the general structure that has proven effective for me. When it comes to file names, you may wish to follow a file naming convention dictated by the client or follow an internal file naming convention, which indicates the project, type of media, asset number, and version number, for example, PROJECT_A_001_01.

If there are multiple courses for one project, you may also want to add an arbitrary course number to keep tabs on which asset belongs to which course. Once a file naming convention has been determined, these file names will be managed within a spreadsheet, housed within the main `200>Media` folder.

The basic goal of this recommended folder structure is to organize your course assets and break them into three groups to further help with the organization.

If this folder structure sounds like it might be functional for your purposes, go ahead and download a ready-made version of the folder structure.

Storyboarding and rapid prototyping

Storyboarding and rapid prototyping will likely make their way into your development glossary, if they haven't already, so they're important concepts to discuss when it comes to streamlining your development. Through experience, you'll learn how each of these concepts can help you become more efficient and this section will discuss some benefits and detriments of both.

Storyboarding is a process wherein the sequence of an e-learning project is laid out visually or textually. This process allows instructional designers to lay out the e-learning project to indicate screens, topics, teaching points, onscreen text, and media descriptions. Though, storyboards may not be limited to just those elements. There are many variations. However, the previously mentioned elements are most commonly represented within a storyboard. Other elements may include audio narration script, assessment items, high-level learning objectives, file names, source/reference images, or screenshots illustrating the anticipated media asset or screen to be developed.

The good thing about storyboarding is that it allows you to organize the content and provides documentation that may be reviewed prior to entry into an authoring environment. Storyboarding provides subject matter experts with a great opportunity for ironing out textual content to ensure accuracy and can help developers in terms of reducing small text changes once in the authoring environment. These small changes are just that, small, but they also add up quickly and can quickly throw a wrench into your well-oiled, efficient, development machine.

Storyboarding also has its downsides. It is an extra step in the development process and may be perceived, by potential clients, as an additional and unnecessary expense. Because storyboards do not depict the final product, reviewers may have difficulty in reviewing content as they cannot contextualize without being able to see the final product. This can be especially true when it comes to reviewing a storyboard involving complex branching scenarios.

Rapid prototyping on the other hand involves working within the authoring environment, in this case Articulate Storyline, to develop your e-learning project, slide by slide. This may occur in developing an initial prototype, but may also occur throughout the lifecycle of the project as a means for eliminating the step of storyboarding from the development process.

With rapid prototyping, reviewers have the added context of visuals and functionality. They are able to review a proposed version of the end product and, as such, their review comments may become more streamlined and their review may take less time to conduct. However, reviewers may also get overloaded by visual stimuli, which may hamper their ability to review for content accuracy. Additionally, rapid prototyping may become less rapid when it comes to revising complex interactions.

In both situations, there are clear advantages and disadvantages, so a best practice should be to determine an appropriate way ahead with regard to development and understand which process may best suit the project that you are authoring.

Streamlining your development

Storyline provides you with so many ways to streamline your development and if you flip to the `Appendix`, *Streamlining Your Development*, you can read about some of them. A sampling of topics discussed includes the following:

- Setting up auto-save
- Setting up defaults
- Keyboard shortcuts
- Dockable panels
- Using the format painter
- Using the eyedropper
- Cue points
- Duplicating objects
- Naming objects

Summary

This chapter introduced you to the concept of pushing Articulate Storyline 2 to its limits, provided you with some tips and tricks when it comes to best practices and being mindful of reusability, identified a functional folder structure and explained the importance that organization will play in your Storyline development, explained the difference between storyboarding and rapid prototyping, and gave you a taste of some topics that may help you streamline your development process. You are now armed with all of my best advice for staying productive and organized and you should be ready to start a new Storyline project!

Now that we've addressed the elephant in the room, *-ahem-* organization *-ahem-*, your development process should run like a well-oiled machine. In the next chapter, you will be provided with a refresher of key concepts such as preparing a story, adding content, adding interactivity and extending slide content, adding visual and auditory media, assessing your learners, and working with slide properties.

2
Refresher of Key Concepts

Now you may already be familiar with the basic development functions of Articulate Storyline, but just to make sure we've covered the basics, this chapter will provide you with a refresher of the key concepts.

These key concepts will allow you to prepare your story for bigger and maybe even better things. Once you understand the primary functions of Storyline, you will easily be able to apply more complex functions across your e-learning project to make Storyline bend to your will!

The purpose of this book is to get you comfortable with pushing Articulate Storyline to its limits. Doing this may also broaden your imagination, allowing you, in turn, to push your creativity to its limits.

There are so many things you can do within Storyline, and a lot of those features, interactions, and functions are often overlooked because they just aren't used all that often or a client project doesn't require them. Often, the basic functionality overshadows the more advanced functions for the following reasons:

- They're easier
- They often address the need
- They take less time to learn and implement

That's understandable, but this book will attempt to open your mind to many more things that are possible within Storyline!

In this chapter, we will cover the following topics:

- Preparing a story
- Adding content to your story
- Adding interactivity and extending slide content

- Adding visual media
- Adding audio
- Assessing your learners
- Working with slide properties

Preparing a story

By now, you probably know how to prepare a new story, but you need to be aware of your options. As someone who tends to start from the ground up with my development, **New Project** is usually the selection I make. However, depending on how you prefer to author e-learning, it might be easier to import from a previously built project or template. This comes in handy if you prefer authoring in PowerPoint or if someone else is developing the branding guidelines and/or templates for your project. The point is that you have options, and they are as follows:

- **New Project**: Create your story by starting afresh, with a blank canvas
- **Record Screen**: Record screen content to integrate into a new story
- **Import**: This option allows you to import content previously developed in the following softwares:
    - Microsoft PowerPoint
    - Articulate Quizmaker
    - Articulate Engage
    - Articulate Storyline
    - You are also able to import questions from text files or Microsoft Excel

Another helpful option you may want to consider when preparing your story is to always remember your **Story View**. This is the view you see when you begin a project, and you can toggle to this view from **Slide View** at anytime.

The purpose of reminding you of this option is that it's a great way to lay out the structure of your story. If you're more of a visual person, you may appreciate being able to add and title all of your scenes and slides from this vantage point to provide yourself with greater context of the course as a whole.

Adding content to your story

Content is essential to any story because without it, there would be no story. In this section, you will become reacquainted with all of the basic content features Storyline has to offer, and these features will be expanded upon in later chapters.

Scenes and slides

Your first order of business before you can add content to your story is to begin by adding scenes and/or slides.

Scenes are basically containers that hold a group of slides. As previously mentioned, ahead of development, you may find it easiest to consider the content you plan on authoring.

Slides are where your content is housed. You will use slides to house the content that users will navigate through. With slides, you are able to define layouts, create the content, and set the content up as you would like it displayed in the final Storyline file. Slides in Storyline work the same as slides in Microsoft PowerPoint, so if you're familiar with Microsoft PowerPoint, you already have the skills you need! If you're not familiar with Microsoft PowerPoint, you're going to catch on quickly; just hang in there!

To add a new scene, select the **New Scene** icon from the **Home** tab. To add a new slide, select the **New Slide** icon from the **Home** tab in either **Story View** or **Slide View**. When in **Story View**, ensure you first select the scene in which you want to add the new slide.

Once slides have been added, you are then able to change the layout, if necessary. You can do this in **Slide View** by right-clicking on the slide you wish to change, clicking on **Layout**, and selecting the desired layout.

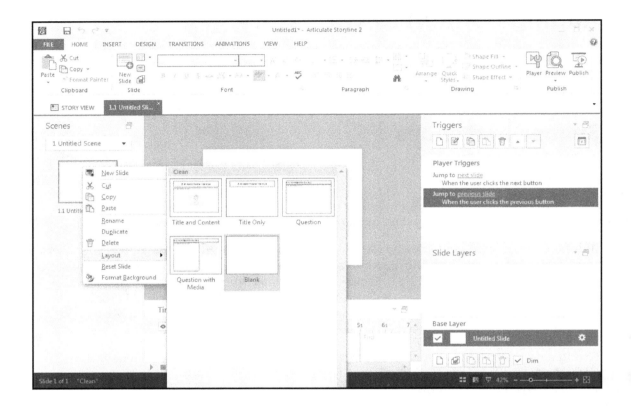

 If you have imported content from another Storyline file or template, you will see all available layouts used in that file within the **Layout** section.

Working with text

If you're familiar with most authoring tools (such as Microsoft Office), even though they aren't e-learning authoring tools, you are probably familiar with all of the capabilities of the internal text editor. Most editors allow you to change font style, size, color, alignment, and more. The text editor in Storyline is no different.

The text you choose to edit can be any slide text, including the text inserted into the slide notes panel, where most text editing options are functional.

However, between Storyline 1 and Storyline 2, the text editing features were enhanced. Storyline 2 allows paragraph alignment/direction, special characters (such as em dashes), and character spacing. If you're a Storyline developer who likes control, you'll be cheering, I know. This functionality allows use to have full control of the text in our stories and make it look just how we want it to look.

Formatting text

Formatting text in Storyline is the same as in any other text editor—you highlight the text you wish to format and use the formatting options as you wish. It is worth noting that the text formatting functionality in Storyline 2 is much more comprehensive than most other text editors. For example, with paragraph spacing, you can now adjust paragraph indentation and line spacing between paragraphs!

To format paragraphs, select the text you wish to format and click on the expand icon in the **Paragraph** section of the **Home** ribbon:

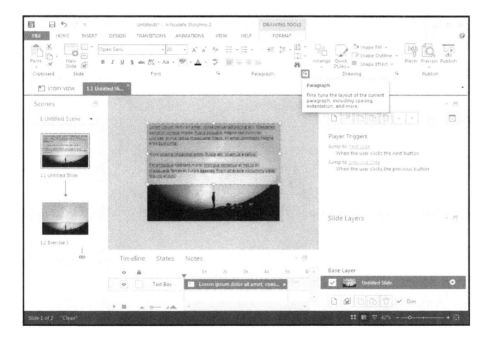

You will be presented with the **Paragraph** menu, where you can adjust alignment, direction, line spacing, and paragraph spacing. In this menu, you can set the available parameters to the desired amounts and select **OK** to apply.

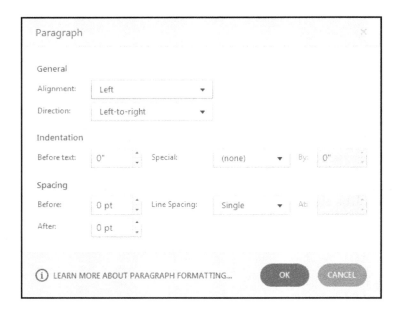

Exercise 1

In this exercise, we'll be focusing on formatting paragraphs. This exercise illustrates just how easily you can control your paragraphs:

1. Click on the text placeholder, where it says **Click to add text**. Type =Lorem() and then press *Enter*. You will notice that sample text has been populated in the text box.
2. With your mouse, highlight all of the text and click on the expand icon on the **Paragraph** menu of the **Home** tab.
3. In the **Paragraph** menu, adjust all variables as indicated in the following list:
   - **General**:
     - **Alignment: Left**
     - **Direction: Left-to-right**
   - **Indentation**
     - **Before text: 0.25″**

- **Special**: Hanging
- **By**: 1.25″
- **Spacing**

  - **Before**: 0.5 pt
  - **After**: 0.5 pt
  - **Line Spacing**: Exactly
  - **At**: 14.25 pt

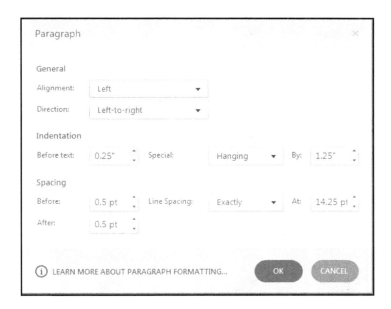

4. Your exercise slide should have progressed from the **Before** slide to the **After** slide in the `Exercise 1` file:

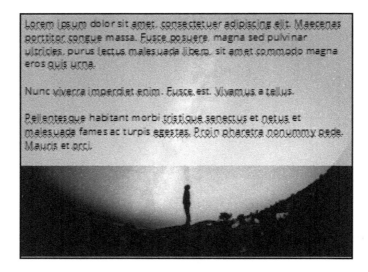

Before slide

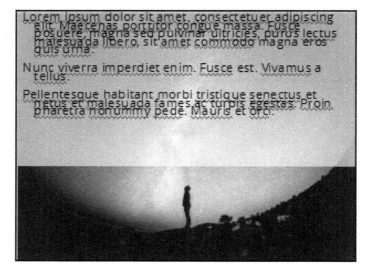

After slide

Adding interactivity and extending slide content

Interactive learning is a pedagogical approach that tends to emphasize interactivity as a means of engaging learners instead of having them passively absorb information. Instead of sitting on a desk and listening to an instructor drone on, filling the brain (the bank) with knowledge, learners are encouraged to engage with the course content by using interactive elements to discover or reinforce their knowledge.

Loosely, interactivity in e-learning may be viewed as anything that requires the learners to interact with components within a lesson, module, or course. Storyline provides a wealth of options when it comes to adding interactivity to your stories, such as buttons, markers, motion path animations, and sliders, just to name a few.

Extending slide content is just as it sounds—extending the content on the main slide, without having to use multiple slides to convey the same information. In Storyline, you have many options for easily extending slide content, such as using layers, scroll panels, or markers, just to name a few.

Some options for extending slide content can also be considered interactive elements. For example, the use of scroll panels requires learners to use their mouse to scroll through textual or visual content. Some other examples of interactivity used to extend slide content could be buttons that trigger additional layers or markers used to highlight areas on a screen and reveal additional content.

Regardless of how you wish to add interactivity to your story, Storyline has functions to meet most all of your interactivity needs.

Working with slide layers

Slide layers are a great way of extending slide content without having to create a new slide. These layers act as an extension of the base layer, essentially layering on top of the base slide layer. We'll be talking a bit more about layers in Chapter 3, *Creating a Content-Rich Story*, so this section will serve to jog your memory about layer basics.

Using the **Slide Layers** panel, you can easily add, duplicate, copy, paste, or delete layers. If you want to extend your base layer content by adding additional content, you can create a new layer that houses the additional content. In the following example screenshot, you will see that three layers, in addition to the base layer, have been created, and these layers contain additional information on the topic being discussed:

In order to get these layers functioning, you will need to apply triggers, which will be discussed next.

Working with triggers

Triggers allow you to set behaviors and dictate how a slide object behaves. You can apply triggers to most slide objects, and most elements of interactivity in Storyline will require trigger application.

You can easily create, edit, copy, paste, delete, and sequence triggers using the **Triggers** menu:

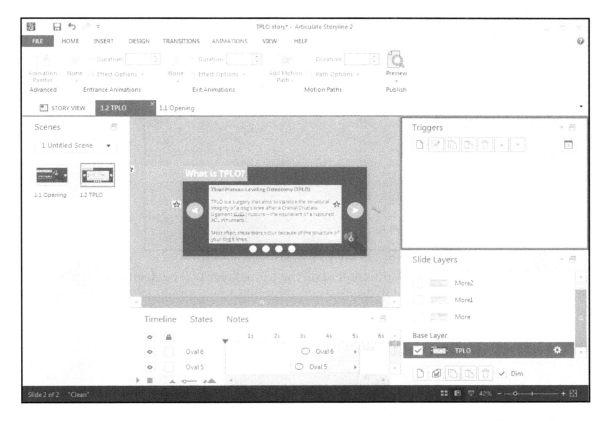

Let's go back to the slide layers we created. In the preceding screenshot, you'll notice there are no triggers. In order for the content in these layers to be displayed, we'll need to add some triggers. In this case, the triggers will be applied to the circular buttons below the main block of text in the screenshot.

To do this, you'll want to select the desired, circular button and create a new trigger. The **Trigger Wizard** will appear, and you will want to specify the **Action** (**Show layer**), the **Layer** (in this case, **More**), **When** the action will occur (when the **User clicks**), and the **Object** that will initiate this action (**Oval 3**), as shown in the following screenshot:

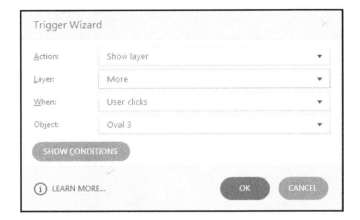

When the user clicks on **Oval 3**, the content on the **More** layer will be displayed. We'll discuss triggers in greater detail in Chapter 4, *Engaging Your Learners with Interactivity*.

Working with states

States are a function in Storyline that provides slide objects with some more pizzazz than just staying in the normal, static, state. Within Storyline, you can create your own states and control these states using triggers or you can use the built-in states that Storyline provides.

Built-in states can be a huge time saver, and Storyline has 10 built-in states:

- Normal
- Hidden

Hidden is a built-in state in Storyline 2

- Hover
- Down

- Visited
- Selected
- Disabled
- Drop Over
- Drop Correct
- Drop Incorrect

 Characters have their own collection of built-in states to change expressions.

These states can be used without having to program triggers to change the state. One example is the **Selected** state. When the user clicks on the object that has the **Selected** state, you will see the result dictated by the state. Again, this is just a refresher. You'll be exploring in more detail the topic of states in Chapter 3, *Creating a Content-Rich Story*.

Exercise 2

Let's take a look at Exercise 2. In this exercise, we'll be creating a custom select state for the oval-menu slide objects. This exercise illustrates how to easily add new states using the built-in states:

1. On the Exercise 2 slide, click on **Oval-Menu1** and then select **States** (between **Timeline** and **Notes**) to view the **States** menu. You'll notice there is only one state: **Normal**.
2. We will be creating a new state. To do this, select **Edit States** and then select the **New** icon; the **Add** state menu will appear.
3. From the drop-down menu, choose **Selected** and click on **Add**. Your **Selected** state will be added. It will look the same as the **Normal** state until you style it.

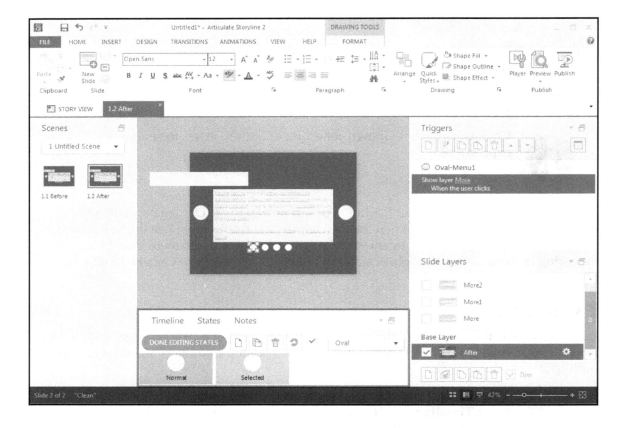

4. From the **Format** tab, style the shape however you prefer, and when finished, select **DONE EDITING STATES**.

5. In this exercise file, we have four oval-menu shapes. So to apply the same **Selected** state to all four oval-menu shapes, simply select the oval-menu shape that already has the **Selected** state applied, and from the **Home** tab, select the **Format Painter** and click on an oval-menu shape that *does not* have the **Selected** state applied.

6. Your exercise slide should have progressed from the **Before** slide to the **After** slide in the Exercise 2 file. When you preview your slide, you should see the oval-menu shapes change formatting when selected. If you preview the **After** slide, you will see that when selected, the oval-menu shapes change color.

Adding visual media

Adding visual media can help captivate your audience, appeals to visual learners, and can help make monotonous content more engaging. In Storyline, visual media includes images, characters, videos, embedding web objects, or adding screen recordings.

If you choose to visually appeal to your audience, Storyline has got you covered!

Here, we'll briefly discus adding images and characters, and then we'll dive into the deeper trenches of adding video and screen recordings in `Chapter 3`, *Creating a Content-Rich Story*.

To add images, simply click on the **Picture** icon on the **Insert** tab. You can then browse for the desired image. Once added, you are able to format your image using the **Format** tab or by right-clicking and selecting **Format Picture...**. When you do this, the **Format Picture** menu will appear and you can modify the image to your liking. If you achieved an undesirable effect when formatting your image, from the **Format Picture** menu, you can select **Reset Picture**, and your image will return to its original state.

Storyline also comes with some built-in characters, in two options: illustrated and photographic. Adding a character is simple. Go to the **Character** menu on the **Insert** tab, choose either **Illustrated Character** or **Photographic Character**, and the **Character** menu will appear.

For **Illustrated Character**, you will need to make several selections from the **Character** menu: **Character**, **Expression**, **Pose**, and the character's **Perspective (Left/Front/Right)**.

For **Photographic Character**, you will make the following selections from the **Character** menu: **Character**, **Pose**, and the character's **Crops (Headshot/Torso/Full)**.

Once you've selected your character, click on **Insert**, and your character will be added to your slide. All characters are scalable, so you can adjust their size once they've been inserted on the slide. You can also edit the character using the **Character Tools** menu on the ribbon, changing the character, pose, expression, or perspective for **Illustrated Character**, and changing the pose or crop for **Photographic Character**.

Adding audio

Incorporating audio into your story will appeal to auditory learners, enhance accessibility (when used in combination with textual elements), and add some personality and realism to otherwise lifeless content.

Storyline allows you to easily import, record, and edit audio files. We'll go into further detail about using audio in Storyline in Chapter 3, *Creating a Content-Rich Story*. So, for now, we'll just jog your memory in relation to how easily you can add audio files to your project.

To insert audio, you will select **Audio** from the **Insert** tab, and you will have two options:

- **Audio from File...**
- **Record Mic...**

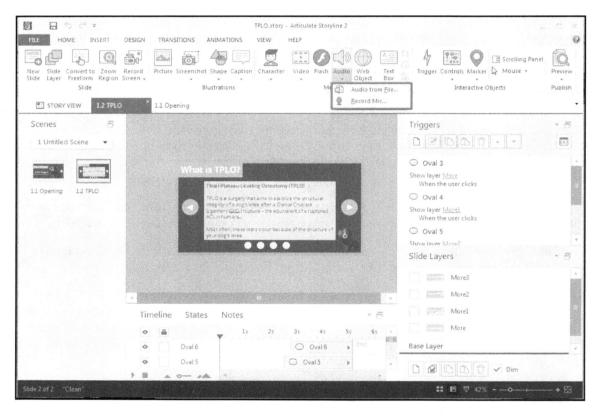

To add audio from a file, select **Audio** from the **Insert** tab and then select **Audio from File...**. You can then browse for the desired audio file and select **Open**.

To record audio, select **Audio** from the **Insert** tab and then select **Record Mic...**. You will then be presented with the **Record Microphone** menu, where you can record, playback, rewind, and delete recorded audio.

You can also set up narration to read from by adding your narration to the **Notes** panel of your slide.

Assessing your learners

Assessing your learners is an essential element of any e-learning project. Most often, you want to ensure that your audience has learned what you have taught them in the program, course, or module you developed. If you're not assessing the learning, how will you know if your e-learning course was effective?

Storyline has multiple options when it comes to assessing your learners' knowledge, and most of this information will be found in `Chapter 6`, *Assessing Learners*. For now, we'll just discuss assessments in Storyline at a very high level to refresh your understanding of question basics.

Working with questions

Storyline has multiple question types. You can select a question type, modify it using the **Form View**, and preview it using the **Slide View**. To insert a question slide, select **New Slide** from the **Insert** tab, click on the **Quizzing** tab, and then choose either **Graded** or **Survey**.

You can also use the shortcut *Ctrl + M* to bring up the **Insert Slides** menu.

To view the available options for graded quiz slides, choose **Graded** from the **Quizzing** tab. To view the available options for survey quiz slides, choose **Survey** from the **Quizzing** tab.

Once you've decided on a question type, simply select **Insert**. The slide will be inserted into your story and you will be able to edit the question accordingly using **Form View** or **Slide View**. In **Form View**, you can specify your question, choices, correct response, and feedback. In this view, you can also specify points per correct or incorrect response, and these points can be modified to suit individual project requirements. For example, if the pass mark is 80% and you have 10 questions, you may want to ensure each correct response is set to achieve 10 points while the incorrect response is set to achieve 0 points.

Form View is a new feature in Storyline 2 that allows you to toggle between the **Form View** and **Slide View**. In Storyline 1, once you select **Insert**, the question form will appear.

Once you've specified your question, answer choices, and feedback (if any), you can toggle back to **Slide View** to see how the question will appear in your course.

When you switch to **Slide View**, you will notice that there is a **Player Trigger** already set up to submit the interaction when the user clicks on the **Submit** button. This functionality helps automate the question-building process and streamline your workflow, but you will need to modify this **Player Trigger** if you want the user to submit in a manner other than clicking on the **Submit** button.

Working with slide properties

In Storyline, you can easily adjust slide properties on a slide-by-slide basis. This will allow you to customize slide behavior and how your learners navigate the story. Specifically, you can adjust how the player advances (automatically or by the user), what behavior occurs when learners revisit a slide (**Automatically Decide / Resume Saved State/ Reset to Initial State**), and which player controls are available.

You can adjust slide properties from **Story View** or **Slide View** (or from question banks, but more on that in Chapter 6, *Assessing Learners*).

To adjust slide properties in **Story View**, select the slide you want to adjust and edit the properties in the **Slide Properties** panel.

In Storyline 1, this is referred to as the **Slide** panel.

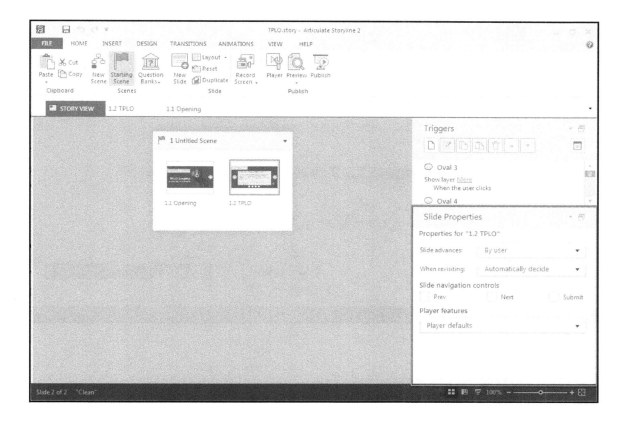

To adjust slide properties in **Slide View**, select the gear icon on the base layer, and the **Slide Properties** panel will appear.

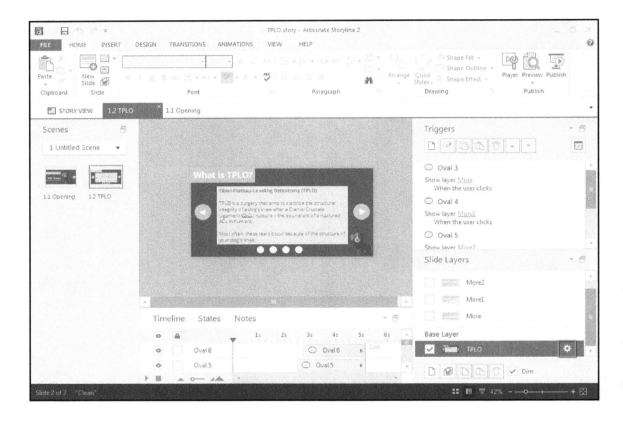

Summary

This chapter reviewed the basics of Articulate Storyline by providing an overview of its key functions. Each of these functions will be discussed in further detail in the upcoming chapters.

Now that you have reviewed the basics, you should be ready to expand your knowledge set and learn how to take these Storyline features and functionalities to the next level. In the next chapter, you will learn helpful tips and tricks for creating a content-rich story, including some *hacks* for current Storyline functionality, and you will begin to apply your basic understanding of Storyline in a more advanced context.

3
Creating a Content-Rich Story

Now that you're reacquainted with basic features and functionality of Articulate Storyline, we're going to delve deeper into the world of creating a content-rich story. In this chapter, you will learn how to harness the power of these basic features and functionality and how to use them in more advanced applications.

Creating a content-rich story is essential as it helps engage learners and optimize organization by extending slide content and provides learners with an opportunity for small amounts of interactivity.

This chapter will give you a taste of interactivity while prepping you for the next chapter where interactivity is at the forefront of discussion! Throughout this chapter, you'll learn some useful tips and tricks.

In this chapter, we will cover the following topics:

- Extending display content
- Adding video to your story
- Adding screen recordings
- Adding audio to your story
- Adding web objects

Extending display content

Display content can be referred to as any content you display on a slide. Extending display content involves employing methods to include more content on one slide, without overwhelming your audience. This last part is important, especially when you're creating educational materials.

There are several methods for extending slide content and we will discuss each method in detail. You may already be accustomed to some of these methods; however, I am confident you'll find a tip or two along the way that will help you turn your design and development into more of a well-oiled machine!

Working with layers

Layers might be considered to be one of Articulate Storyline's fundamental elements. Some may even put them right up there next to the likes of triggers. If you have ever worked with graphic design programs, such as Adobe Photoshop, you will understand the importance of layers. If you have no previous experience with layers, you are in for a treat!

Layers are just what they sound like—they allow you to build content on top of content and are a great way to reduce screen count. Layers have many of the same properties as slides. In my experience, layers have been used to create tabbed-style interactions to display content in smaller-scale branching scenarios, to create interactive timeline interactions, and to create unique navigation opportunities.

One of the reasons that layers are such an important element in Storyline is that they easily allow you to extend your display content in response to specific triggers, but I digress. We will talk more about triggers in Chapter 4, *Engaging your Learners with Interactivity*. Triggers aside, there are several things you need to know about working with layers.

All slides consist of a **Base Layer**, which is the primary layer you populate with content. However, you can add a new layer by selecting the **New Layer** icon in the **Slide Layers** panel or by selecting **Slide Layer** from the **Insert** tab. These new layers allow you to populate additional content, just as you would by adding a new slide:

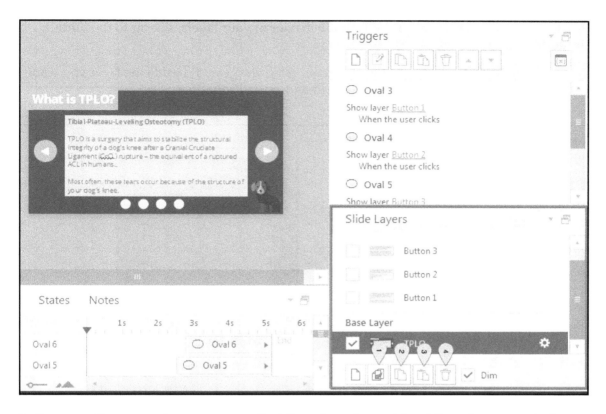

In the preceding example, you can see that there have been at least three layers created (**Button 1**, **Button 2**, and **Button 3**) in addition to the **Base Layer**. Each of these layers will reveal more information about the main slide topic. Therefore, by adding these layers, we were able to remove the necessity of adding each of these content layers as new slides, which would increase the slide count of your entire story.

Within the **Slide Layers** menu, you can also see that you have the ability to duplicate (**1**), copy (**2**), paste (**3**), and delete (**4**) selected layers; you can even rename layers (by double-clicking on the current layer name) or change their position in the **Slide Layers** menu (by clicking and dragging it to the desired position).

A sometimes overlooked feature of layers is **Slide Layer Properties**. These properties allow you to further customize the visibility and behavior of your layers, similar to the **Slide Properties** menu.

To access the **Slide Layer Properties** (**2**) menu, select the gear (**1**) beside the layer you want to work on or right-click on the desired layer and select **Properties**.

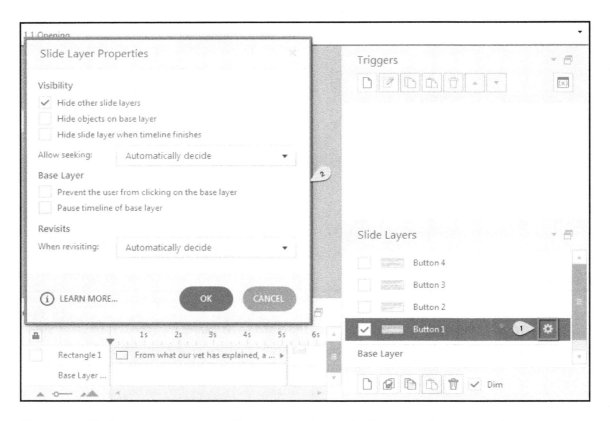

Here we will discuss what each of the options shown in the preceding screenshot do:

- **Hide other slide layers**: This option hides all other layers when the current layer is visible, with the exception of the base layer. This is a default selection because most often developers only intend for one layer to be shown at a time. However, if you have an interaction that builds on each layer, you will want to deselect this option.

- **Hide objects on base layer**: This option hides all objects on the base layer. This is a great option if you have objects on the base layer that will obscure the information being presented on a layer; however, you should be cognizant of the fact that if you have created buttons for other layers or custom navigational elements on the base layer, these will disappear when the layer is selected.
- **Hide slide layer when the timeline finishes**: This option closes the slide layer when the timeline finishes. This is a great option if you have audio/video and want the user to return to the base layer when it ends.
- **Allow seeking**: This option dictates whether the user can use the seekbar on the layer. You can choose either **Automatically decide** (which is the default),**Yes**, wherein the seekbar would be active for the layer, or **No**, wherein the seekbar will not be active on the layer, but it will still be visible from the base layer (it just won't do anything).
- **Prevent the user from clicking on the base layer**: This option prevents the user from interacting with elements on the base layer. Again, you will want to be conscious of this if you have custom navigational elements on the base layer.
- **Pause timeline of base layer**: This option pauses the timeline of the base layer when the specified layer is visible. This option allows the user to pick up where they left off (with the base layer) when the specified layer is closed. With audio, you will want to be careful when selecting this option as it may make your base layer audio seem disjointed.
- **When revisiting**: This option allows you to dictate the behavior of the layer when the user revisits or reopens the layer. You can specify whether it will **Automatically decide**, whether it will reset to initial state (which I would recommend for most interactions), or whether it will resume saved state (pick up where the user left off).

 Because the **Hide objects on the base layer** function hides all of the objects on the base layer, you may want to go a different route if you only want to hide certain objects on the base layer. To do this, you will want to select the expand icon (**1**) on the timeline and then deselect the eye icon (**2**) on the relevant object you wish to hide from the base layer.

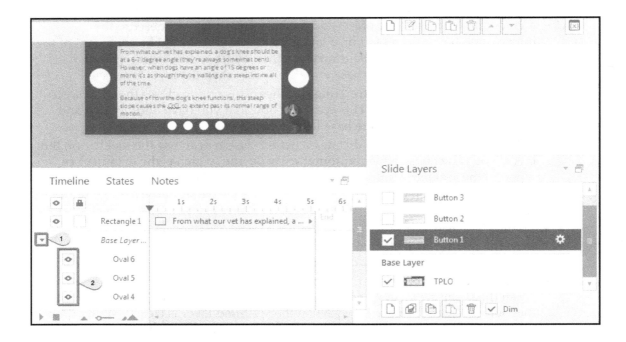

Working with states

As we discussed in Chapter 2, *Refresher of Key Concepts*, states are a function in Storyline that jazz up slide objects versus maintaining their normal state. Storyline provides built-in states (all objects have a **Normal** state, which is the way an object looks when it is inserted onto the slide, and buttons have a number of in-built states), but this section will be primarily concerned with creating custom states. States allow you to easily inject interactivity into your story by changing the appearance of an object based on user interaction.

First, we will talk about the basic functionality of states and then you will learn how to leverage the full potential of states to create some neat interactions!

States can be applied to most objects on a slide, such as images, shapes, text boxes, and, in Storyline 2, the next and previous buttons too. You can change the appearance of states, including the built-in states, by using the standard formatting functionality. You can also add objects or effects to the states, such as images (for example, check marks), animations, or audio.

The short and sweet of how states work is that you select the slide object you wish to add a state to, access the **States** panel by selecting **States**, select **EDIT STATES** and, then either add a new state or modify an existing state.

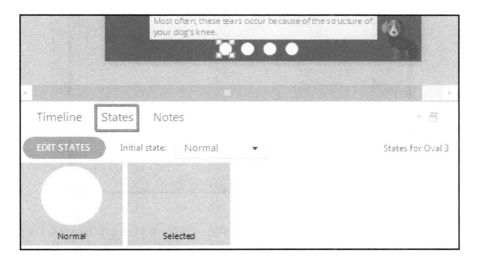

If you are creating a custom state, you will need to add your own triggers to make the state change functional, but the built-in states will have triggers already associated with them, more on triggers is covered in Chapter 4, *Engaging Your Learners with Interactivity*.

Within the **States** panel, you can **EDIT STATES**, and within **EDIT STATES**, you are able to create new states, duplicate states, delete states, or reset states.

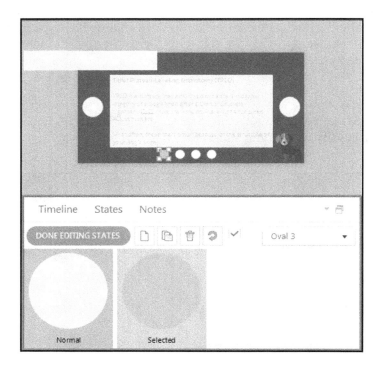

Once you have your initial object state created, you can use the Format Painter tool to copy the format of the completed object, including its states, to other objects.

That's the basic gist of how to use states and, because you're reading this book and not one of its predecessors, it's pretty safe to assume you're looking to learn how to do some cooler things with states, so here we go!

Creating a toggle button effect

Toggle buttons are great because they allow you to easily move (or toggle) between two options, which comes in handy when you're trying to enhance some of your static course content.

Now, you can create this effect using sliders, which we will discuss further in Chapter 4, *Engaging your Learners with Interactivity*, but for a simple two-point toggle (for example, off and on), it might be more efficient to create the effect using states.

This example was inspired by Jeff Kortenbosch's e-learning challenge entry in the Articulate E-Learning Heroes Community; refer to `https://c ommunity.articulate.com/series/45/articles/toggle-switch- and-slide-your-way-to-more-creative-buttons`.

Exercise 1

Let's take a look at Exercise 1. In this exercise, you will learn how to create a two-point toggle button using states. This exercise illustrates just how easily you can create an interactive two-point toggle button!

1. On your blank screen, you will want to create a container for your toggle button. To do this, you will want to add a shape to the slide. In this example, we have used a rounded-rectangle shape that is 43px in height and 115px in width.

2. Then, you will want to create the toggle button. To do this, you will want to add a shape that is the same (or less) height as your container and a little less than half the width of the container. In this example, we have used a rounded-rectangle shape that is 43px in height and 50px in width.
3. This smaller shape will be your default toggle button. Because this example is illustrating **Off** and **On**, format the shape to be red and add the text `Off`.

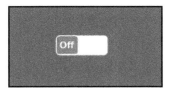

4. Now, click on the smaller red shape and select your **States** panel. You will see that there is a **Normal** state already in the **States** panel. This is the default state.

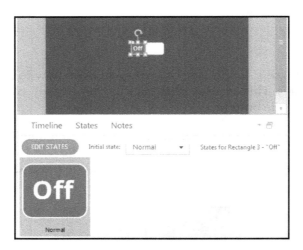

5. Select **EDIT STATES** and then select the **New State** icon. Enter `Selected` as the new **State name** and click on **ADD**.

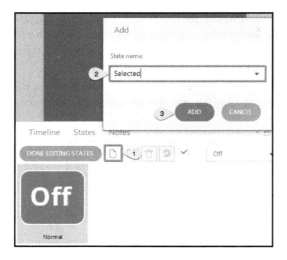

6. You will now see a new state, **Selected**, that looks identical to your **Normal** state. Using the **Format** menu, change the shape color to green and then replace the **Off** text with text that reads **On**. You will then want to move the shape to the other side of the container using the right-arrow key on your keyboard. Your Exercise 1 slide should now look similar to your Exercise 1 **After** slide.

7. Because we are using one of Storyline's built-in states, there is no need to add additional triggers. The selected state is activated when the user clicks on the object, so, when you preview this slide and click on the red **Off** shape, your green **On** shape will activate. Then, if you click on the green **On** shape, the red **Off** shape will activate.

When to use layers versus states

In some situations, layers and states can serve similar functions and it can be hard to decide which approach to take. Here you will find some recommendations to help make your decision easier.

It's best to first consider what you need your slide objects to do. States can best be used to make slide objects change, whereas layers can be used to display different or additional slide objects or information.

A huge determining factor is whether you need to house interactive components that require triggers. If you do, your decision is easy since you cannot add triggers to objects within a state, so you will need to use layers.

If you are creating an interaction that requires simple tracking, states might be a better option as layers tend to require variables for simple tracking, such as whether the learner has selected all options before moving on to the next slide. In this example, it would be much easier to apply a visited state to each relevant object than it would be to add variables to each relevant layer.

Another consideration comes from a development perspective. If multiple developers are working with or will be working with a Storyline file, the use of states for something you could conceivably use layers for might be confusing and not overtly visible to another developer. For example, if you're using a **Selected** state to reveal learning objectives, other developers might be looking for layers when they go in to modify this slide. So, unless you specifically explain this functionality, other developers may unnecessarily spend time trying to figure out how you programmed a particular slide.

Creating a Nested Menu Effect

The next example will start with states and end with variables, triggers, and hotspots, so we will set up the nested menu in this exercise and then complete the functionality portion of the menu in `Chapter 5`, *Using Variables, Conditions, and JavaScript*.

 This example was originally shared by Josh Stoner in the Articulate E-Learning Heroes Community; refer to `https://community.articulate` `.com/articles/how-to-create-a-cool-menu-button-nesting-an` `imation-effect-with-storyline`.

Exercise 2

Let's take a look at Exercise 2. In this exercise, you will learn how to create a really neat looking nested menu effect.

1. To begin, you will want to create a shape, format it to your desired colors and font and add a + symbol.

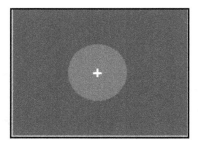

2. Then, you will want to duplicate the shape by pressing *Ctrl + C* and then *Ctrl + V*. Ensure you position the duplicated shape over top of the initial shape and remove all formatting (no fill, no outline, and no effect) from the duplicated shape. Your slide should look as it does in the following screenshot, the initial shape with a dashed box around it:

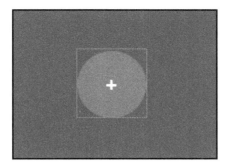

3. Once you have the visible shape and the invisible shape, reposition and rename these shapes on the timeline. You will want the invisible shape to be at the bottom of the timeline and the visible shape at the top of the timeline. Name the visible shape `Icon` and name the invisible shape `Animation`.

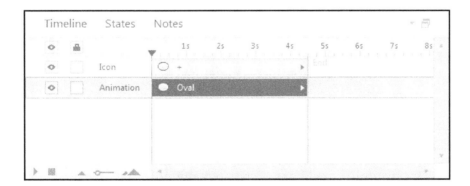

4. Now, set up your menu items. In this example, there are three polygon shapes with numbers (**1**, **2** and 3). Once satisfied with the menu items, select all of them at once and cut them from the base layer by pressing *Ctrl + X*. Select the **Animation** shape and toggle to the **States** panel. Select **EDIT STATES** and, on the **Normal** state, press *Ctrl + V* to paste the cut menu items.

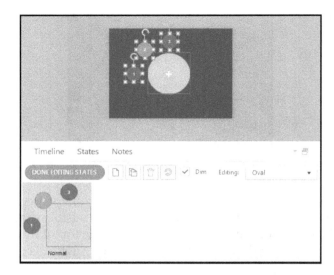

5. From the initial **States** drop-down menu, select **Hidden**, and then select **DONE EDITING STATES**.

6. Return to the **Timeline** panel and select the **Animation** shape. From the **Animation** tab, change **Entrance Animation** from **None** to **Grow** and change **Exit Animation** from **None** to **Shrink**. Because the menu items are nested within the **Animation** shape's state, the entrance and exit animations will be automatically applied to them.

7. Next, we are going to create four layers. The first layer will be titled Menu Hotspots, and from the **Insert** tab, you will select **Controls** and then choose the circular hotspot. You will draw a hotspot around each of the menu items.

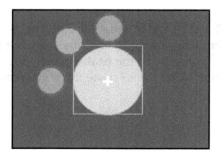

8. From the initial **States** drop-down menu, select **Hidden** and then select **DONE EDITING STATES**.

9. On the next three layers, you will create a rectangle along the bottom of the slide and enter some placeholder text. In this example, rectangles of different color were used for different menu items.

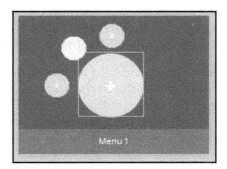

10. That's all we're going to do at this point, but keep this exercise file handy because you're going to learn how to make this nested menu work in `Chapter 5`, *Using Variables, Conditions, and JavaScript.*

Working with hotspots

Storyline provides another avenue for extending slide content and that is through the use of hotspots. Hotspots are invisible shapes that trigger a user response. They can be used to add interactivity by making part of an image or slide clickable. A trigger is automatically applied to each hotspot, but you will need to customize the trigger to get the hotspot to behave the way you want it to.

To add a hotspot, select **Controls**, select the hotspot shape (**oval, rectangle**, or **freeform**), and draw the hotspot on the slide.

One more *advanced* way of using hotspots in terms of unique interactivity is to apply them to videos to create an interactive video. We will be talking about that concept a little more later on when we start exploring video functions in Articulate Storyline.

Working with lightboxes

Lightboxes are a great way of extending slide content without needing to program the content into a specific layer on an existing slide. This works particularly well when creating custom *pop quiz* style elements, navigation overviews, or course/module **Frequently Asked Questions** (**FAQs**).

Lightboxes are slides which, when activated (by a trigger), present content in an overlay on top of the current slide. When a lightbox is active, the current slide behind the lightbox is dimmed and a close button is automatically built into the lightbox.

You can also add lightbox slides to player tabs, so if you want to display course navigation or FAQs from the player instead of within the course slides, you have options! To add a lightbox slide to the player, select the **Player** button from the **Home** tab. The **Player Properties manager** will appear and, from the **Features** tab, you will want to select the **New** icon below the **Player Tabs** section.

A **Trigger Wizard** will appear and you will want to define the name of the tab, where you want the tab to align on the player and, under **Action**, you will choose **Lightbox Slide**. At this point, you can also specify whether you want to include navigation controls; however, it is advisable to refrain from including these controls as it might cause confusion between the lightbox navigation controls and the course navigation controls. You will then select the slide you want to appear in the lightbox and when the lightbox will appear (for example, on a click).

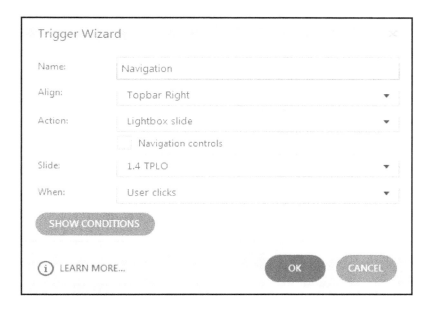

Once you select **OK** and preview your project, you will see that the tab has been added to the player. When you select the tab, the lightbox slide will appear.

You can change the color of the exit button by accessing the **Cascading Style Sheet** (**CSS**) information in your output. Please note that this will only work with HTML5 content. The file you are looking for is `player.css` and it is typically located in the `mobile` folder of the published output. When you locate this file, open it in a text editor, such as notepad, and search for `f00`; you will find the window close icon section of the CSS. You will want to change `f00` to your desired color hex code.

Working with scrolling panels

Scrolling panels are the epitome of extending slide content as they provide a container to which you can add additional content, which would otherwise overflow past the slide size.

While most instructional designers may tell you that scrolling is just a bad design idea and not to even think about doing it, sometimes it's necessary and scroll panels really make it easy to avoid slide after slide of scrolling and instead you might be able to just consolidate all of the content within one scrolling panel!

To add a scroll panel, all you have to do is select **Scrolling Panel** from the **Insert** tab and then draw it where you want it to exist on the slide.

You can also do some neat things with scrolling panels, like create an automatic scroll panel or a horizontal scroll panel.

Exercise 3

Let's take a look at Exercise 3. In this exercise, you will learn how to create the effect of an automatic scroll panel.

1. To create this effect, the first thing you will want to do on your exercise slide is to create a scroll panel within the gray rectangle in the center of the slide.
2. Then, you will want to add a text box with a width slightly smaller than the scroll panel, above or below the scroll panel. You will populate this with some text by typing =Lorem() and hitting *Enter*.
3. Now, drag the text box into the scroll panel. With the text box still selected, select the **Add Motion Path** button from the **Animation** tab and then select **Lines**.
4. Once the motion path has been added, you will specify the following parameters under the **Path Options** drop-down menu:
   - **Direction**: **Up**
   - **Easing Direction**: **None**

5. Once you have made these specifications, you will need to ensure that the start point of the motion path (the green arrow) is near the bottom of the scroll panel and not below it (or your text will appear to be starting outside of the motion path). The endpoint of the motion path (the red arrow) is near the top of the scroll panel and not above it. You can change these point locations by clicking and dragging the point to the desired location.

6. You will then need to change the **Duration** as this will ensure that the text does not move too quickly in the scroll panel. In this example, we have set the duration at 15 seconds.

7. Finally, you will want to amend the trigger, if necessary. When you add a motion path, Storyline automatically adds a trigger to move the motion path when the timeline starts. If, however, you want a bit of a delay, you will need to change the trigger so that the motion path moves when the timeline reaches X. In this example, we amended the trigger to begin moving the motion path when the timeline reaches 0.5 seconds.

8. Your exercise slide should now look similar to the after slide and, when you preview your slide, your text should appear to be scrolling automatically within the scroll panel!

Exercise 4

Let's take a look at Exercise 4. In this exercise, you will learn how to create a horizontal scroll panel.

 Please note that these instructions are for use in Storyline 2.

This effect is a neat one to use if you want to include a running ticker tape across the bottom of your slide (think Stock Exchange or News Broadcast). You can provide *breaking* information to your learners or use this effect to display tips and tricks.

1. To create this effect, the first thing you will want to do on your exercise slide is create a scroll panel within the yellow rectangle at the bottom of the slide and extend the width slightly past the slide width. Doing this will ensure that the scroll bar is not visible on your ticker.

2. Then, you will want to add a text box ensuring that the width is much wider than the scroll panel. The key to this effect is ensuring that all of your text fits on one line, so if you have a lot of text, you will want to add an incredibly wide text box.

3. Now, drag the text box into the scroll panel. With the text box still selected, you will select the **Add Motion Path** button from the **Animation** tab and then you will select **Lines**.

4. Once the motion path has been added, you will specify the following parameters under the **Path Options** drop-down menu:
   - **Direction**: **Left**
   - **Easing Direction**: **None**

5. Once you have made these specifications, you will need to ensure that the start point of the motion path (the green arrow) extends to the furthest right of the yellow rectangle, or past it and that the endpoint of the motion path (the red arrow) is at the furthest left of the yellow rectangle. As in the previous example, you can change these point locations by clicking and dragging the point to the desired location.

6. Finally, you will want to amend the trigger, if necessary. In this example, we amended the trigger to begin moving the motion path when the timeline reaches 2 seconds.

7. Your exercise slide should now look similar to the after slide and, when you preview your slide, your text should begin, at 2 seconds, scrolling horizontally across your slide.

Adding video to your story

Video is a great way of adding engagement and personality to any story and Storyline provides many options for adding video. First, we'll discuss some of the basics of adding video files and then we'll talk a bit more about doing some neater things with video in Storyline, such as ideas for creating interactive video.

Another great thing about Storyline when it comes to video is that it offers built-in video editing functionality, so you can perform basic video editing. Once you have added a video to your story, you can access the **Video Editor** by double-clicking or selecting the video on the slide and also from the **Video Tools** tab and then selecting **Edit Video** option.

Within this video editor, you can trim or crop the video, adjust audio volume, adjust video brightness/contrast, insert a logo, or change/reset the video. For a software product that isn't a video editor, Storyline does pretty well at providing you with most of the features you would need to quickly and efficiently edit your own videos internally.

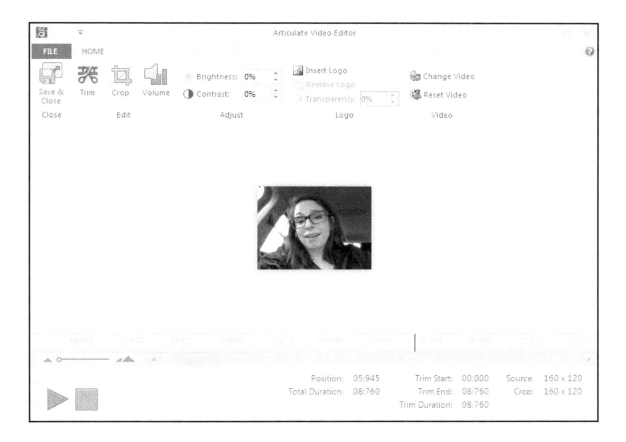

Adding videos from a file

Adding a video from a file is very straightforward. All you have to do is select **Video** from the **Insert** tab, then select **Video from File** from the drop-down menu, browse for the video file you wish to add to the slide, and select **Open**.

Adding videos from the Internet

Storyline also provides you with the ability to add video files from the Internet. To do this, you will need to select **Video** from the **Insert** tab and then select **Video from Website**. The **Insert Video from Website** window will appear and you will need to insert the embed code for the video you wish to add.

To locate this embed code, you will usually select the **Share** option on the video and an embed code will be provided.

Once you have entered the video embed code, you will select **INSERT**:

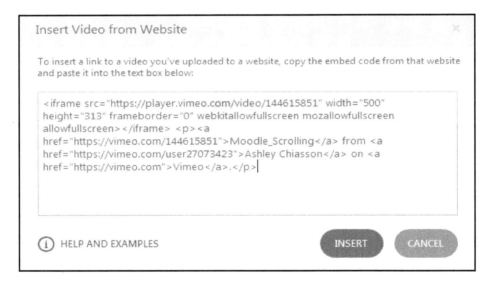

Your video will then appear on the slide and you will be able to preview it just as you would a video added from file:

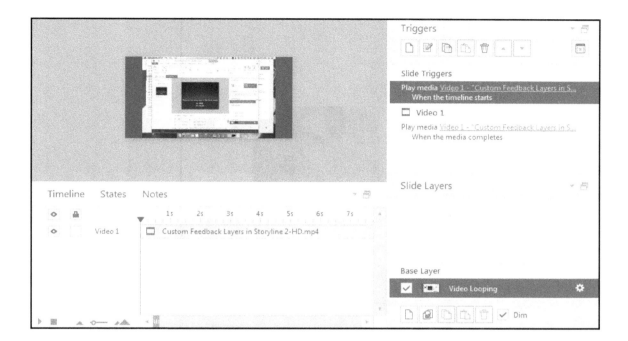

 Please note that when developing for mobile devices, embedding video as a web object is the preferred method.

Recording webcam

In Storyline, you can also add video by recording from the webcam on your computer. A more advanced way of using your webcam recordings within your Story may be to create explainer videos to accompany software simulations you created using the screen record function in Storyline or to accompany existing step-by-step explainer videos. Doing this may enhance your user's learning experience by providing additional context and a higher level of personalization.

To record from webcam, select **Video** from the **Insert** tab and then select **Record Webcam**. The **Record Webcam** window will appear and you will be able to record, stop, and delete your webcam recordings from this window. Once you are satisfied with the video, select **OK**.

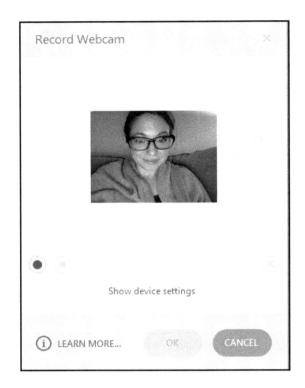

Importing PowerPoint content as video

Another way of adding video is to import Microsoft PowerPoint content as video. This is a useful option if you or a client already have interactions built out in PowerPoint and it is not necessary to recreate these interactions in the Storyline file. This method could be particularly helpful when dealing with complex animated graphs or charts.

First, you will want to export your PowerPoint slide as a video. To do this, you will need to open PowerPoint, create or navigate to the slide you wish to export, select **File**, select **Export**, and then select **Create Video**.

Once you have created the video, you will simply add the video file to your Storyline slide by selecting **Video** and then selecting **Insert from File**.

Adding interactivity within your videos

Interactive videos are a fantastic way of keeping your learners engaged. You can even use interactive videos to ensure that your students are paying attention by forcing them to interact with the videos at various junctures.

Less involved (for your learners) means of creating interactive videos include working with the timeline to have objects appear and disappear on the video at various points throughout the timeline. In this context, it might be helpful to have markers appear throughout the video with additional information or have shapes with text containing additional information appear.

The more involved methods of creating interactive video would be having your learners interact with objects that appear on the video, wherein the video pauses until the learner has completed the interaction.

Exercise 5

Let's take a look at Exercise 5. In this exercise, we'll be creating an interactive video that employs user prompts. The video will not resume until the user responds to the prompt in the correct manner.

1. First, you will want to add a video to your slide and, using the play controls on the timeline, hit the play icon until you reach an area in your video that you want to add a prompt or question to; at this point, you will hit the stop icon on the play controls.

2. Move the playhead to the point in your video where you have decided you want to add a prompt. In this example, we have decided on 3.25 seconds as our stopping point.

3. At this new point, add a rectangle or text box and type the text you want to use for your prompt or question. In this example, we have asked the user to click on the head of the giraffe on the left.

4. Then, you'll want to add a new trigger to the rectangle that specifies the following parameters:
   - **Action**: **Pause Media**
   - **Media**: Your video
   - **When**: **Timeline Starts**
   - **Object**: Rectangle or textbook—whatever you've added your prompt to

5. At this point, you will also add a hotspot by selecting **Controls** and then choosing either the circle, rectangle, or freeform hotspot. Draw the hotspot where you want the user to click.

6. Hotspots will always generate a trigger. Double-click on the hotspot trigger and change the parameters as follows:
   - **Action**: **Play Media**
   - **Media**: Your video
   - **When**: **User Clicks**
   - **Object**: **Hotspot**

7. Innately, the Storyline video functionality allows the user to click on the video, when viewing the published content, to either pause or play the video. Because we want to control when the video pauses and plays, you will need to create another hotspot. For this hotspot, you will select the rectangle and place the hotspot around the entire slide, ensuring it spans the entire duration of the timeline. Leave the trigger unassigned.

8. Lastly, you will need to ensure that the first hotspot moves up in the timeline so that it appears over the second hotspot. To do this, simply drag hotspot 1 up to the top of the timeline.

9. Your exercise slide should now look similar to the after slide or the following screenshot:

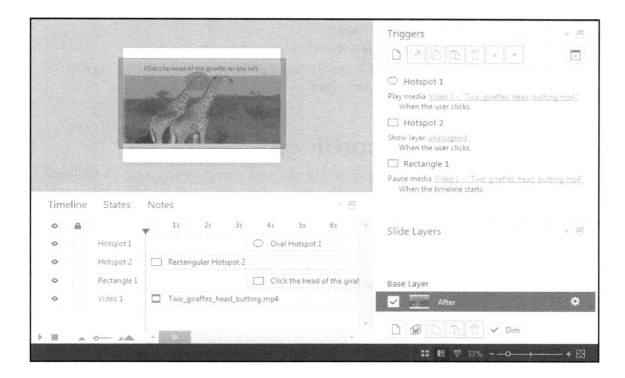

Looping slide video

Looping is an effect developers look for when they want to insert background video or audio; it's very easily achieved in Storyline and can be done in just a few steps:

1. First, you will need to insert your video or audio file into a slide.

2. Then, you will need to add a second trigger with the following parameters; this trigger will tell your media to begin playing again:
   - **Action**: **Play Media**
   - **Media**: Your video or audio
   - **When**: **Timeline Starts**
   - **Object**: The slide

3. Then, you will need to create a trigger with the following parameters, this trigger will tell your media to play:
   - **Action**: **Play Media**

- **Media**: Your video or audio
- **When**: **Media Completes**
- **Object**: Your video or audio

4. Now your video or audio file should begin playing again as soon as the first instance of the media has completed.

Adding screen recordings

Screen recordings are a great way of explaining procedures or detailing complex tasks in a meaningful way and are often used to easily create software simulations. Storyline provides four options for creating a screen recording and you can select the option that fits best with your need.

 Once a screen recording has been added, it can be edited just the same as any video would be using the **Video Editor**. You also have the option of using **Action Fine Tuning** if you need to adjust the start or end frame.

Video mode

In **Video mode**, the screen recording will play like a video. In this mode, the user will only be able to watch the video that has been recording.

To add a screen recording in **Video mode**, select **Record Screen** from the **Insert** tab. When you are ready to record, select the red record button, record what you want to record, and select **Escape** when you are done with your recording.

Once the output has generated, you will want to provide the output with a meaningful name in the **Name** field, select **Insert Video as a single slide**, specify whether you want the screen recording to appear in a new or existing scene, and select **INSERT**. Your screen recording will then be added to the slide as any other video on file would.

 If you want your mouse movements to be recorded, you will want to select **Show mouse cursor**. This is a great way of adding additional context that may be lost by the learner after the initial video view.

View mode

In **View mode**, the user will view the screen recording as a demonstration (as in video mode), but each step along the way will be clearly identified using captions that tell the user what to click and where.

To add a screen recording in **View mode**, you will record the screen as you would in **Video mode** and then specify **Step-by-step slides**, **View mode** steps, specify whether you want the screen recording to appear in a new or existing scene, and then select **INSERT**.

When you select **View mode** options, you can specify caption language, whether you want to include text captions, whether you want to include the mouse cursor, or whether you want to indicate clicks with a highlight.

 Please note that recorded audio will not be included in **View mode** or **Try mode**.

Try Mode

In **Try mode**, the user gets to try each step and will get remediation with each user input; however, their performance is not graded.

To add a screen recording in **Try mode**, select **Record Screen** from the **Insert** tab. When you're ready to record, select the red record button, record what you want to record, and select **Escape** when you're done with your recording.

Once the output has generated, you will want to provide the output with a meaningful name in the **Name** field and then you will select **Insert as:** | **Step-by-step slides**, selecting **Try mode** steps from the drop-down menu. You will then want to select whether you want to insert the slide into a **New Scene** or **New Slide** and identify a scene/slide name.

If you select **Try mode options**, the **Try Mode Options** screen will appear. Here, you can specify caption language, whether you want to show correct feedback, a hand cursor when hovering over hotspots, or caption hints and, if you want caption hints, you can specify how you want them to appear.

 You will want to ensure that, if there are slide master artifacts on your slide layout (for example, placeholder information), you change the slide layout to blank as this will remove those artifacts.

Once you have specified all of the relevant parameters and selected **INSERT**, you will see that Storyline has broken the steps down into separate slides for each main action. Here, you can edit the size of hotspots and the text within hint captions and you can format the color of hint captions however you prefer.

Test mode

Test mode is the same as **Try mode** with one exception—the user is scored and a result slide is produced.

Test mode functions as a graded assessment, so you can assess your user's knowledge of a process within this mode. To add a screen recording in **Test mode**, you'll want to record the screen recording as you would in video, view, and try modes, but then specify the following parameters: **Step-by-step slides**, **Test mode steps**, whether you want to insert the screen recording in a new or existing scene, and then select **INSERT**.

If you select **Test mode options**, you can also specify whether you want to show correct or incorrect feedback, whether you want to automatically create a result slide, how many attempts the user gets to complete the test, and whether you will display the try again feedback.

Alternatively, you can insert a screen recording from another project. However, to do so, you will need to export the project as an MP4 video from the original project and then import it, as video, into the new Storyline project.

Action Fine Tuning

Another great feature that the Storyline screen recordings provide is **Action Fine Tuning**. Action Fine Tuning allows you to update start and end frames of your screen recording; you can access this feature by right-clicking on the screen recording on your timeline and selecting **Action Fine Tuning...**.

This feature comes in handy when you are using hints or captions and you need to adjust the start frame so as not to give away the answer right away. To adjust the start or end frame of a screen recording in Action Fine Tuning, simply drag the start marker to the left or the end marker to the right until the caption or hint is out of view.

If you wish to export screen recordings, you can do so by selecting **Record Screen** from the **Insert** tab. Once the preview window opens, you can right-click on the preview area and either select **Export Video**, which will export the entire screen recording as an MP4 video, or **Save frame**, which will export an individual frame from the screen recording as an image.

Within Action Fine Tuning, you can also right-click on any preview area and select either **Export Video**, which will export a copy of the entire screen recording as a video, **Export Clip,** which will export the current clip as a video, **Save frame (project size)**, which will export an individual frame as an image at the size it appears in your story, or **Save frame (original size)**, which will export an individual frame as an image at the size it was recorded.

Adding audio to your story

Adding audio to your story is a great way of adding a higher level of personalization many projects require audio and you can use less screen text while incorporating additional information in your audio. Storyline provides two ways of adding audio: from file or recorded from microphone.

To add audio from file, select **Audio** from the **Insert** tab, select **Audio from File**, browse for the audio file you wish to add to the slide, and select **Open**.

Recording audio from microphone is a great option for recording scratch audio tracks ahead of a client review. It's also a great option if you have the means for recording professional-grade audio because you can easily act as your own voice-over artist. To record your own audio, select **Audio** from the **Insert** tab and select **Record Mic**. **The Record Microphone** window will appear and here you can record, playback, or delete audio recordings.

 Another great feature of the **Record Microphone** window is that, if you add your audio script to the **Notes** panel of your slide, you can click on the **Narration Script** icon in the **Record Microphone** window and your narration script will appear while you record, negating the need to have an audio script displayed in another application or on another monitor.

Using the audio editor

Much like the video editor, Storyline provides an audio editor that allows you to perform many basic editing functions. To access the audio editor, double-click on the audio file on your slide or right-click on the audio file on your slide, and select **Edit Audio**, or select **Audio Editor** from the **Audio Tools** tab.

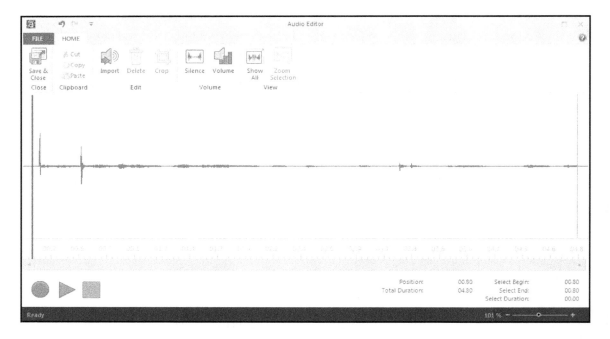

Three handy features of Storyline's audio editor are the following:

- **Import Audio**: This feature allows you to import existing audio files to add to the audio file on your slide. This feature is great when you have a large chunk of audio and only a small amount of the audio needs to be replaced. You can delete the chunk that needs to be replaced and add the newly recorded audio file to fill the gap, reducing the need (and expense) of having to rerecord the entire audio file.

  To do this, click on the area of your waveform where you wish to import new audio, select **Import**, browse for the file you wish to import, and select **Open**.

- **Silence**: This feature allows you to add silence to areas of the existing audio track. This comes in handy if there isn't enough of a pause between parts of speech in the audio track.

  To do this, click on the area of your waveform where you wish to add silence and select **Silence**. The **Insert Silence** window will appear and you can specify your duration (in seconds). Click on **OK**.

- **Delete**: This feature allows you to delete sections of the existing audio track, which becomes helpful when you need to delete sections of the audio file and don't want to rerecord the entire track. It also becomes helpful if you need to delete sections of audio before importing new recordings.

  To do this, highlight the section of audio you wish to delete and click on **Delete**.

Looping slide audio

Creating a looping audio effect in Storyline is the same process as looping video:

1. First, you will need to insert your video or audio file into a slide.
2. Then, you'll need to add a second trigger with the following parameters—this trigger will tell your media to begin playing again:
   - **Action**: **Play Media**
   - **Media**: Your video or audio
   - **When**: **Timeline Starts**
   - **Object**: The slide
3. Then, you will need to create a trigger with the following parameters—this trigger will tell your media to play:
   - **Action**: **Play Media**
   - **Media**: Your video or audio
   - **When**: **Media Completes**
   - **Object**: Your video or audio

Using cue points to streamline audio synchronization

Cue points are one of the biggest time-savers in Storyline and a lot of people either don't use them, don't know they're an option, or don't realize just how much time cue points will save them when it comes to tediously synchronizing slide objects with audio or video.

Creating cue points is easy! First, you'll need to have your media (audio or video) loaded on your slide. Then, using the timeline playback controls (**1**), select the play icon. Let your media play through and, anytime you hear or see an area where you want to have a slide object (for example, text boxes, shapes, and so on) appear, hit *C* on your keyboard.

Once you have created all of your cue points, you can right-click on any object on your slide, mouse over **Align to Cue Point** (**2**), and select the cue point (**3**) you wish to align the slide object.

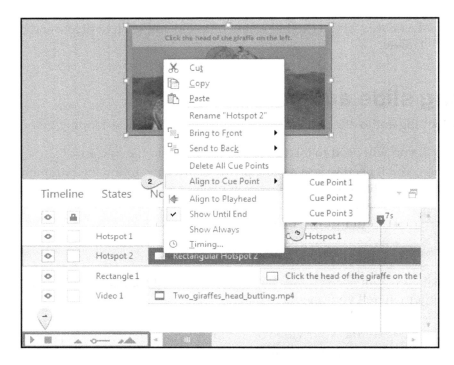

This process is so much less tedious than manual synchronization, especially if you have a project that deals with a lot of audio!

Adding web objects

Web objects are any web content, such as websites, blogs, forums, external videos, or flash files. Storyline lets developers add web objects to their slides, either by linking the web object within the slide or by displaying the web object in a new browser window.

When working with web objects, you will be unable to preview the web object until the story has been published and uploaded. It will not display locally.

To add a web object, select **Web Object** from the **Insert** tab. The **Insert Web Object** window will appear. Here you will specify the link to the web object, how you want the web object to display, and how the web object should behave. Once you have specified these parameters, select **OK** and the web object will be inserted onto your slide.

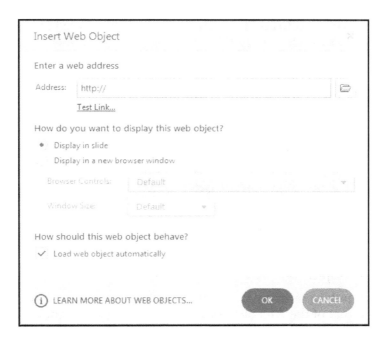

One great way of using web objects is to create an embedded PDF viewer effect. This is a fairly easy effect to create and allows the learners to review PDF documentation within the slide without having to leave the course or module to access the content in another location, such as a local Intranet.

You can also layer content on top of web objects by using the timeline. This process will likely be a bit more tedious because you won't be able to use cue points in the same way you could if you were importing your own audio or video. This is because you are unable to preview the web object prior to publishing.

 You can still use cue points, but you will need to watch the external video, pause it whenever you want to layer a slide object, and then go back in to the slide and add cue points manually by right-clicking on the timeline, move the playhead to the desired location, right-click, and select **Create Cue Point At Playhead**.

Exercise 6

Let's take a look at Exercise 6. In this exercise, you'll learn how to create an embedded PDF viewer effect. We will be using a lightbox to display the PDF viewer as the built-in exit button will come in handy, so students don't need to navigate away from the current slide.

1. First, you will need to add the web object to your sample PDF slide in the exercise scene. To do this, select **Web Object** and specify the following parameters:
   - **Address:**
   - **Display in slide**
   - Check **Load web object automatically**

2. When you select **OK**, you will see that your web object has been added to your slide. At this point, you can make any necessary sizing adjustments.

3. Next, you will need to trigger the lightbox slide to appear. To do so, navigate to the PDF prompt slide of the exercise scene. Select the text box **Click for Sample PDF** and click on the add new trigger icon. Set up your trigger using the following parameters:
   - **Action**: **Lightbox Slide**
   - **Slide**: **1.2 Sample PDF**
   - **When**: **User Clicks**
   - **Object**: **Text Box 1**

4. Once you publish and upload your content, your exercise slide should appear similar to that of the after slide or to the following screenshot:

Summary

This chapter took some of the basic concepts of creating a content-rich story and provided you with some recommendations for how you can easily begin to push these basic concepts to the next level by creating more complex interactions.

You learned many ways of extending display content using layers, states, hotspots, lightboxes, and scroll panels and also learned how to add and enhance your video by incorporating interactivity. You also gained knowledge about the four available screen recording modes and how to use them, how to add and edit audio using Storyline's built-in audio editor, and how to do some neat things with web objects, such as adding a PDF viewer to a slide and how to layer content on top of web objects.

Now that we've identified how you can create a very robust story using various content functions within Storyline, you should be ready to learn a bit more about the interactive features specific to Storyline and how to integrate them with what you've learned in this chapter.

In the next chapter, you will learn how to do some cool things to make your stories more interactive. Specifically, we will show you the ins and outs of how to use motion paths, animation options, and the animation painter.

4
Engaging Your Learners with Interactivity

Now that you understand ways in which Storyline can help you grab your learner's attention, you're ready to knock their socks off by doing some really cool things, which will make sure to keep their attention! In this chapter, you will learn how to create interactivity using essential elements, such as triggers, and other Storyline functionality, such as buttons, markers, sliders, and animations.

The purpose of this chapter is to show that you can easily keep your audience engaged with your story by providing them with sample opportunities to interact with the story's content. Very few people enjoy passively learning and filling their brain with content, with no opportunity to apply the newly learned information. Instead, you will learn how Storyline can easily provide your learners with the ability to be a part of your story.

This chapter will show you how to apply the concept of interactivity in an easy and logical manner. With many opportunities to follow along, you will surely learn something that you can put to use in your next project! Remember, you will always have the activity files to fall back on if you need to dig deeper into the interaction to understand exactly how it works.

In this chapter, we will cover the following topics:

- Working with triggers
- Doing neat things with buttons and markers
- Working with slider interactions
- Adding animations
- Using the zoom region to create interactivity
- Working with triggers

In Chapter 3, *Creating a Content-Rich Story*, we discussed how layers were considered one of Articulate Storyline's fundamental elements. Another fundamental element is triggers.

Triggers allow you to make things happen, literally. Creating a trigger for an object will allow you to make that object interactive in some manner. This is why this functionality is considered fundamental in Articulate Storyline! Triggers will help you to engage your learners by bringing your story to life.

The type of interactivity triggers allow is conditional in that triggers are programmed with dependent variables. You can add triggers to most objects, bending those objects to your will, well, at least in terms of what actions triggers are capable of dictating. Most of your projects will be laden with triggers, so it's really important that you understand what they're capable of doing.

First off, triggers are programmed from the **Triggers** panel, on the right-hand side of the Storyline interface, by clicking on the **Create a new trigger** icon or by clicking on an object on the slide and selecting **Trigger** from the **Insert** tab. The **Trigger Wizard** will appear—get used to this **Trigger Wizard** because you're going to spend a lot of time here.

Within the **Triggers** panel, you can do the following:

- Create a new trigger (**1**)
- Edit a selected trigger (**2**)
- Copy and paste a selected trigger (**3**)
- Delete a selected trigger (**4**)
- Reposition an existing trigger up or down in the list of triggers (**5**)
- Manage story variables (**6**)

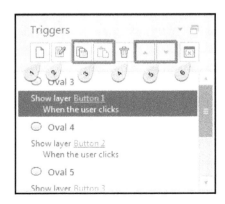

Adding triggers

Within the **Trigger Wizard**, you can dictate the *what*, *where*, and *when* of a trigger. This occurs in phases of drop-down boxes within the **Trigger Wizard**.

Defining the Action

When you select **Action** from the **Trigger Wizard**, you will be able to choose from all available actions. Storyline has 24 actions, which are broken into five subgroups: **Common**, **Media**, **Project**, **More**, and **Quiz**:

Defining where the Action occurs

Depending on the **Action** you choose, the next drop-down menu will be one of many options; this is when you will select the *where* for your trigger:

- **On Object**: This appears when the action is **Change State of** and is used to specify which object you want to change the state of.
- **Layer**: This appears when the action is **Show Layer** or **Hide Layer** and is used to specify which layer you want to show or hide.
- **Slide**: This appears when the action is **Jump to Slide** or **Lightbox Slide** and is used to specify which slide you want to jump to or which slide you want to open in a lightbox.
- **Scene**: This appears when the action is **Jump to Scene** and is used to specify which scene you want to jump to.
- **Media**: This appears when the action is **Play Media**, **Pause Media**, or **Stop Media**, and is used to specify which media object you want to play, pause, or stop.
- **Object**: This appears when the action is **Move** and is used to specify which slide object you want to move. Please note that the **Move** action is associated with motion path animations.
- **Variable**: This appears when the action is **Adjust Variable** and is used to specify which variable you want to adjust.
- **Timeline**: This appears when the action is **Pause Timeline** or **Resume Timeline** and is used to specify which timeline you want to pause or resume.
- **File**: This appears when the action is **Jump to URL/File** and is used to specify a URL or file that you want to jump to. Please note that within this submenu, you can browse for a file, check a file or URL, and adjust browser settings.
- **Email**: This appears when the action is **Send Email To** and is used to specify a recipient e-mail address.
- **Script**: This appears when the action is **Execute JavaScript** and is used to enter JavaScript code.
- **Interaction**: This appears when the action is **Submit Interaction** and is used to specify which interaction you want to submit.
- **Results**: This appears when the action is **Submit Results**, **Review Results**, **Reset Results**, or **Print Results**, and is used to specify which results slide you want to submit, review, reset, or print.

Defining when the Action occurs

Once you've chosen the *what* and *where* of your trigger, you will need to specify the *when*. Within the **Trigger Wizard**, you will be able to choose from 17 options, which are broken down into four groups: **Click Events**, **Timeline Events**, **Drag Drop Events**, and **Other Events**:

- **User Clicks**: The action will occur when the user clicks on an object.
- **User Double Clicks**: The action will occur when the user double-clicks on an on object.
- **User Right Clicks**: The action will occur when the user right-clicks on an object.
- **User Clicks Outside**: The action will occur when the user clicks on outside of an object or objects.
- **Timeline Starts**: The action will occur when the timeline starts.
- **Timeline Ends**: The action will occur when the timeline ends.
- **Timeline Reaches**: The action will occur when the timeline reaches a specified time.
- **Object Dragged Over**: The action will occur when an object is dragged over another object or objects.
- **Object Dropped On**: The action will occur when an object is dropped on another object or objects.
- **User Presses a Key**: The action will occur when the user presses a specified key. Another field will appear when you choose this option and you will be able to specify the desired key at this point.
- **State**: The action will occur when the state of an object or objects is as specified. With this option, you will be able to specify whether you need the state of multiple objects to change (**All of**), the state of any specified objects to change (**Any of**), or the state of none of the specified objects to change (**None of**). You will be able to select the necessary objects and then specify whether the object(s) **Is** or **Is Not** a specified state (you can choose the desired state from the drop-down menu).
- **Variable Changes**: The action will occur when a specified variable changes. With this option, you will be able to specify the relevant variable.
- **Mouse Hovered Over**: The action will occur when an object is hovered over. You will also be able to specify whether you want the object to restore when the mouse is no longer hovered over the object.
- **Media Completes**: The action will occur when the specified media completes.
- **Animation Completes**: The action will occur when the specified animation completes.

- **Control Loses Focus**: The action will occur when the user is doing nothing with the mouse and/or keyboard.
- **Slider Moves**: The action will occur when the slide moves to a specified condition. This option is used when working with sliders in Storyline and you will be able to specify the **Condition** (**None, < Less Than, > Greater Than, <=Less Than or Equal to, >= Greater Than or Equal to, == Equal to,** or **!= Not Equal to**).

The next step in the **Trigger Wizard** is to specify which slide object will activate the action. For example, if the **Action** is **Jump to Slide**, you might want the user to click on a specific button before the slide changes.

Once you've programmed all applicable trigger fields, you can click on **OK** and be done with the trigger or you can take things one step further and program conditions for that trigger.

To add a condition to your trigger, select **SHOW CONDITIONS** in the **Trigger Wizard**:

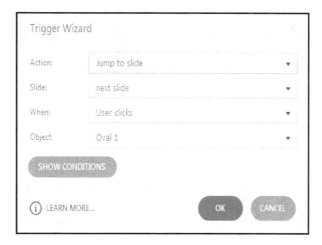

The **On Condition** menu will appear. Here, you can either **HIDE CONDITIONS**, add a trigger condition, edit a trigger condition, or delete a trigger condition.

Conditions allow your trigger to *work* only when specified criteria are met. Trigger conditions work with variables, shapes, or windows. Because we have not yet discussed variables, we will focus this explanation on shapes.

You can add multiple trigger conditions to a trigger.

To add a new trigger condition, select the **Add Trigger Condition** icon. The **Add Trigger Condition** menu will appear. Here, you will select **Shapes**. You will see that there are **If, Operator**, and **State** fields.

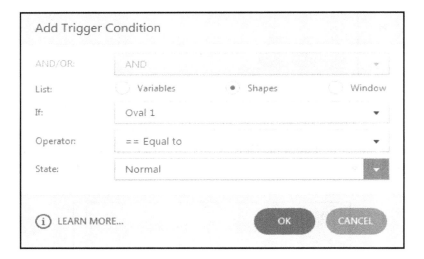

The **Shapes** conditions work alongside **States**. To program a **Shapes** condition, you will first choose the slide object from the **If** field (in this case, **Oval 1**), then you will select the **Operator**, which will be **== Equal to** or **!= Not Equal to**, from the **Operator** field, and then you will select the state from the **State** field.

In the preceding screenshot, we are telling the trigger to occur if **Oval 1** is equal to the **Normal** state.

When it comes to the **Window** condition, you can choose to have the trigger occur in two instances:

- If the slide is inside the player frame
- If the slide is lightboxed

Once a trigger has been added, you can copy a trigger by using the copy/paste icons in the **Triggers** Panel or by copying and pasting the slide object, which already has triggers added to it. These triggers can be copied from one slide and pasted to another slide and come in handy—particularly when you have a project setup with complex triggers.

Editing triggers

Editing a trigger is just as easy as adding a trigger. You can either double-click on the trigger in the **Triggers** panel or select the trigger and click on the **Edit** icon. In both instances, the **Trigger Wizard** will appear. You can make your changes and click on **OK** to close the **Trigger Wizard**.

Alternatively, if a trigger is visible in the **Triggers** panel with blue underlined text, you can edit that trigger by clicking on the blue underlined text and selecting another option. In the next screenshot in the *Exercise 1* section, you will see that Button 1 and Button 2 are in blue underlined text. In this example, when you click on the text, the other available layers will appear for selection (for example, Button 1, Button 2, Button 3, and Button 4).

Exercise 1

Let's take a look at Exercise 1. In this exercise, you'll learn how to create triggers to control display layers sequentially. Each of the buttons will be disabled unless the state of the button previous to it has been selected:

1. On your exercise slide, if you select any of the circles below the content box and toggle to the **States** panel, you will notice that there is already a **Selected** state and a **Disabled** state. You will also notice in the **Triggers** panel that there are already triggers to show layers when the user clicks on each button.
2. In order to create the conditional interactivity, you will want to click on **Oval 4** (the second circle from the left) and add a new trigger. In the **Trigger Wizard**, program the trigger as indicated in the following screenshot, and click on **OK**:

3. Next, click on the trigger you just created and select the copy icon on the **Triggers** panel. Then, click on **Oval 5** and select the paste icon on the **Triggers** panel. Your **Triggers** panel should now look like the following screenshot:

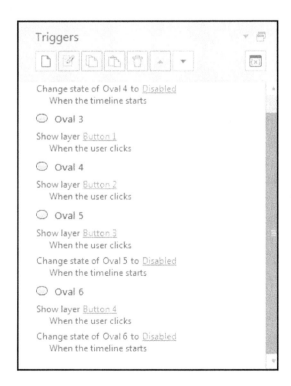

4. Now, we want to program the trigger to change the state of **Oval 4** to **Normal** when **Oval 3** is in the **Selected** state. Basically, we don't want the users to be able to navigate to the next content until they have visited the previous content (no jumping ahead!). To do this, select **Oval 4** and add a new trigger. Here, we will be programming the trigger and the condition. Your trigger should be programmed as shown in the following screenshot:

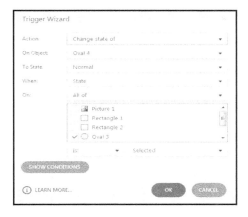

5. You will repeat the last step until **Oval 4**, **Oval5**, and **Oval6** all have triggers applied, indicating when they will change states to **Normal**.

6. When you preview your exercise slide, you should now be unable to click on the third and fourth buttons. The second button will be active for selection. If you are having difficulty in achieving this effect, take a look at the **After** slide and troubleshoot where you went wrong. You're likely just missing a trigger!

Doing neat things with buttons and markers

Among Storyline's built-in functions are buttons and markers. These two elements provide you with the ability to easily inject interactivity within any story, with minimal effort.

Buttons provide an easy way of creating functional activity within any story. You can use Storyline's built-in buttons or create your own using shapes. You can even create customized previous and next buttons and disable the default player buttons! Buttons are used along with triggers to create actions, typically when the user clicks on the button.

Markers are a great way of enhancing your screen real estate by acting as a container for additional information that is only presented when the learner interacts with the marker (for example, hover the mouse over or click on the marker).

Buttons

Under **Controls** on the **Insert** tab, Storyline has several built-in button options, including two standard buttons in rectangle and oval shapes, four checkbox styles, and four radio button styles. The rectangle and oval buttons, when added to a slide, are pre-built with trigger functionality, and all buttons, including checkboxes and radio buttons, have built-in states. Of course, all of these elements can be further customized if you wish to do so.

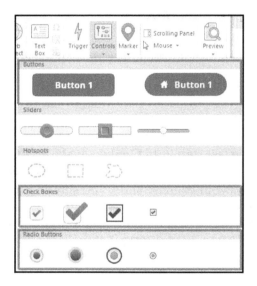

You can add buttons in two different ways:

- Selecting **Controls** on the **Insert** tab, choosing the appropriate button, and drawing the button onto your slide.
- Creating a custom button by selecting **Shape** on the **Insert** tab, choosing an appropriate shape, drawing the shape onto your slide, and then adding a trigger to the shape.

You can add text to your button if you're using the default buttons (oval and rectangle) or if you're using a custom shape. All you have to do is click on the button or shape and start typing the desired text.

You can even add icons to your button by accessing the **Button Tools Format** tab and selecting the appropriate icon. Alternatively, if the icon you're looking for is not available from the **Button Tools Format** tab, you can create your own by inserting the icon as a picture, moving it over the button or shape, selecting both the picture and the button/shape, and grouping these two elements together by right-clicking and selecting **Group**, or by pressing *Ctrl + G*.

To delete a button, all you have to do is right-click on the button and select **Cut**, or select the button and press *Ctrl + X*.

Button sets

Button sets are a magical, and sometimes overlooked, function of Storyline in that they make slide objects respond as though they are radio buttons. Radio buttons allow the user to select only one object at a time; therefore, button sets allow users to select only one object at a time. When an object is selected, all other objects become deselected.

This feature comes in handy when you want to create custom quiz objects or if you want to include multiple quiz questions on one slide (think Likert scale questions or true/false questionnaires). Because button sets allow users to only select one object within the button set, this makes them ideal for adding multiple questions to one slide without having to do tedious programming.

To create a button set, you will first want to design your slide with all relevant slide objects. Then, select all of those objects, right-click, and select **Button Set** and then **New Set...**:

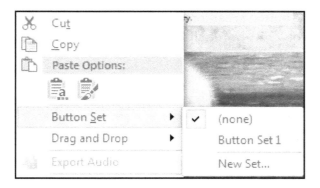

You will be prompted to enter a **Name** for the **Button Set**. To do so, click on **Add**. The **Button Set** will then be created. If you preview the slide, you will see that all objects you had selected to add to the button set are no longer static; they're selectable, but you can only select one object at a time.

The objects in your button set will automatically have a selected state added to them. You can edit the selected state just the same as you would edit any other state.

Exercise 2

Let's take a look at Exercise 2. In this exercise, you'll create a button set from existing slide objects:

1. First, preview your exercise slide and hover the mouse over options **A**, **B**, **C**, and **D**. You will notice that your cursor does not change, indicating that the objects are selectable. Now close the slide preview.
2. Select all of the rectangles containing option letters **A**, **B**, **C**, and **D**.

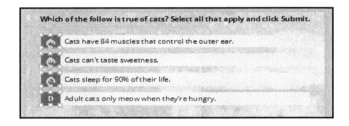

3. Next, right-click, select **Button Sets**, select **New Set**, type in a name for the button set, and click on **Add**. At this point, if you toggle to the **States** panel, you will also notice that the button set automatically added a **Selected** state.
4. Now when you preview the slide, you will see that your cursor has changed, indicating that the objects are selectable. You may select the objects, but only one at a time.

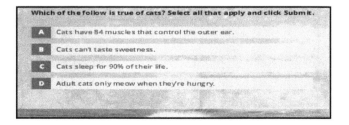

5. Your exercise slide should now look like the **After** slide.

Exercise 3

Let's take a look at Exercise 3. In this exercise, you'll create button sets from existing checkboxes to allow the user to make selections for multiple questions on one slide. With checkboxes, you must add button sets to prevent the user from clicking on multiple responses to a single question.

1. First, preview your exercise slide and click on the checkboxes. You'll notice that you're able to select any of the responses, regardless of whether you've already selected a response for that statement.

2. In order to prevent users from selecting multiple responses to one question, you will add a button set to each question. To do this, you will select all of the checkboxes for a particular statement by clicking on each of them while holding the *Ctrl* button.

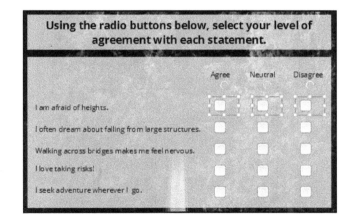

3. Then, as in the previous exercise, you will right-click, select **Button Set**, select **New Set**, name the button set (I used Q1, Q2, and so on), and click on **Add**. Do this for all questions.

4. Now, when you preview your exercise slide, you should only be able to select one response per statement.

5. Your exercise slide should function like it does in the **After** slide. It should look similar to the **After** slide or to the following screenshot with 5 button sets—one for each question's three potential responses:

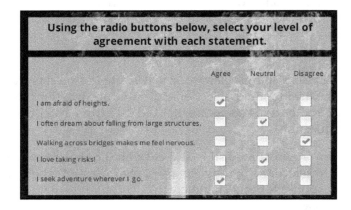

Markers

Markers are another one of Storyline's very handy built-in features that elicit interactivity. They are easy to add and allow you to maximize your screen real estate.

You can easily add a marker to any slide by selecting **Marker** from the **Insert** tab and then selecting any of the available (and many) icons.

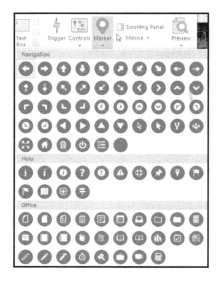

Once you select the marker icon you want to use, simply click anywhere on your slide and the marker will be placed. You can click and drag the marker anywhere you want, so you don't have to worry about placing the marker accurately on the first try.

You will see that your marker has been placed and that a textbox has populated. Here, you can add the additional information you would like to include within the marker.

When you click anywhere else on the slide, you will notice that the text box or media container has collapsed. It hasn't disappeared! To access it again, simply click on the marker.

Markers behave in one of the following two ways:

- **On Hover**: When the user hovers over the marker, the label title will appear. It will disappear again when the user is not hovering over the marker.
- **On Click**: When the user clicks on a marker, the label will appear, and it will only disappear when the marker is clicked a second time or when the user clicks anywhere outside of the marker.

If you wish to change the default behavior, you can do so, but only so much that you have the entire label appear when the user hovers over the marker. This will remove the need for the user to click on the marker.

Within the **Marker Tools Format** tab, you can further customize your markers by changing the icon, adding audio (recorded from a mic or imported from a file), adding media (a picture from file, a video from a file or website, or recorded webcam), and changing the animation, indicating whether you just want audio (and no text), whether you want all to show on hover/mouse over, or whether you want the visual formatting of the marker such as color fill, bored, icon color, and more.

In the music genre example in the preceding screenshot, you might wish to add audio or video samples within your markers, informative explanations, or even a brief recorded webcam *lecture* explaining key points about the genre. Let your imagination run wild and let your learners interact with the slide to learn more about your subject matter!

Another neat thing you can do with markers is create a transparent marker effect that reveals content when various areas of a slide object are hovered over.

 Jerson Campos shared this tip in the Articulate E-Learning Heroes Community and also uploaded a video on YouTube: `https://www.yout ube.com/watch?v=JbU8oke_jmI&feature=youtu.be`.

Exercise 4

Let's take a look at Exercise 4. In this exercise, you'll learn how to create a transparent marker effect to reveal information on hover. This effect will use markers, shapes, formatting, and states:

1. Your exercise slide has been populated with an image of an articulate illustrated character sitting at a desk. In this exercise, we'll be creating a transparent hover effect with markers and states to indicate various office elements, specifically the character's headset, the computer, and the keyboard.

2. To begin, add a marker to your exercise slide near the character's headset. Choose the marker that has no icon. Add the label title **Headset** and reduce the size of the textbox. Your marker should look similar to the following screenshot:

3. Then, with the marker selected, access the **States** panel. Here, you will double-click on the **Normal** state to edit it and you will add a shape around the character's head.

4. Under the **Format** tab, choose **No Outline**, then right-click on the shape, and select **Format Shape**. Here, you will set the **Transparency** to **100%** and click on **OK**. Select **DONE EDITING STATES**.
5. With the marker still selected, access the **Marker Tools Format** tab and select **Marker Fill**: **No Fill**, **Marker Outline**: **No Outline**, and under **Animate**, select **None**. If you preview this slide, you will notice that if you hover over the character's head, the marker appears reading **Headset**, as shown in the following screenshot:

6. Click on **Exit preview** and use the same method to create another marker for **Computer** and another marker for **Keyboard**. Your exercise slide should now appear similar to the **After** slide. When you hover over the character's head, the **Headset** marker will appear; when you hover over the computer monitor, the **Computer** marker will appear; and when you hover over the keyboard, the **Keyboard** marker will appear.

Working with slider interactions

Sliders are a new feature with the release of Storyline 2 and are super versatile! You can use slider interactions to control the movement of slide objects, to reveal additional information, to change character expressions, to illustrate cause and effect relationships, and to create slick toggle buttons. Of course, these are just a few suggestions; you can really let your imagination take control and use sliders however you want to use them!

Interactions such as knob-style dial effects, which previously may have taken hours of programming and hundreds of state changes, can be easily created by simply inserting and programming a slider. Therefore, the slider function in Storyline helps you do neat things that can be impactful for your learners, with minimal programming and effort. You can even have multiple sliders on one slide.

First, we'll talk about how to add and format the sliders and then we'll move on to how to make the slider work:

1. To add a slider to your story, select **Controls** from the **Insert** tab and choose one of the three available slider styles.

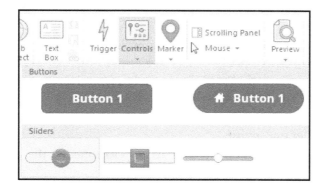

2. Next, click and drag the area on your slide where you want the slider to appear. You will see that the slider has been placed on your slide. The slider comprises two main elements: the thumb (**1**) and the track (**2**). The thumb is what the user will click and drag along the track to reveal view the programmed interaction.

3. In the **SLIDER TOOLS | FORMAT** tab, you can easily customize your slider just as you would any other slide object.

If you're unsatisfied with the look of the thumb or track, you can even change them to an image. You can easily do this by selecting **Thumb Fill | Picture or Track Fill | Picture**, browsing for the relevant image, and importing it as your thumb or track. Here is an example: perhaps your story is about planets and their distance to the sun. You might want to use an image of a galaxy as your track and an image of the sun as the thumb. Those subtle changes would certainly liven up your story!

You will use the **Slider Tools Design** tab to program your slider properties. Here, you will identify the following properties:

- **Variable:** This will change if you have multiple sliders—which slider you're adjusting the properties of
- **Update**: How you want the slider to update; you have two options: while the slider is dragged or when the learner releases
- **Start**: The slider start point
- **End**: The slider end point
- **Initial**: Where you want the thumb to be positioned at the beginning of the interaction
- **Step**: The step in the interaction

Finally, you will need to set up triggers to get your slider to become functional. These triggers will occur when the slider moves. The positions you dictated in the slider properties will become relevant now. For example, if we have a start of 1 and an end of 3, you will need to add two triggers. Your initial point will be the default. Therefore, if your initial point is 1, you will need to set up a trigger for 2 and 3. This will tell the slider that when the learner drags the slider thumb to points 2 or 3, a different interaction will occur.

For example, if you have an illustrated character on your slide, you could use a slider to change the character's expression. On 1, the character might have a neutral expression, on 2, the character might have an alarmed expression, and on 3, the character might have an angry expression. The following is what your **Trigger Wizard** would look like for one of your slider triggers:

Once you have your triggers programmed, your slider will work like a dream!

Exercise 5

Let's take a look at Exercise 5. In this exercise, you'll learn how to use a slider to activate layers. You'll also get to flex some of the new tips you've learned throughout the past few chapters:

1. Your exercise slide has been populated with Atsumi, one of Storyline's most famous photographic characters. It has also been populated with four layers, each containing a different Atsumi pose. The base layer has Atsumi showing one finger, and each subsequent layer shows her counting up (for example, layer two shows two fingers, layer three shows three fingers, and so on).

2. Next, you'll add another trigger with the following parameters:
    - **Action: Jump to Slide**
    - **Slide: 1.1 Exercise**
    - **When: Slider Moves**
    - **Slider: Slider 2** (**Slider 1** is being used on the **After** slide)
    - **Condition: == Equal To 1**

3. The first thing you'll do is add a slider by selecting **Controls** from the **Insert** tab, selecting a slider style of your choosing, and drawing the slider across the top white space on your exercise slide.

4. With the slider still selected, select **Design** from the **Slider Tools** tab and change **Start** to 1, **Initial** to 1, **End** to 5, and **Step** to 1.

5. Now you need to add your triggers. First, add a trigger with the following parameters:
   - **Action**: **Show Layer**
   - **Slide**: **Two**
   - **When**: **Slider Moves**
   - **Slider**: **Slider 2** (**Slider 1** is being used on the **After** slide)
   - **Condition**: **== Equal To 2**

6. Then, for the remaining layers, copy the trigger you just created to **Show layer Two**, paste it, and using the blue underlined links, change **Two** to **Three** and **equal to 2.00** to **equal to 3.00**. Do this for all the remaining layers. Your trigger panel should mimic the following screenshot:

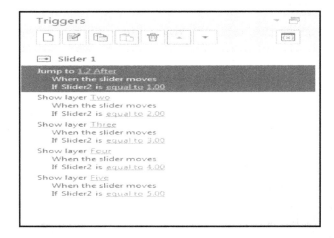

7. When you preview your exercise slide, you should now see Atsumi counting up and down on her fingers as you drag the slider all the way to the right, and then all the way back to the left. Your exercise slide should look similar to the **After** slide.

Adding animations

Animations are a great way of enhancing your story by adding a bit more pizzazz to your slide objects. You can make extensive use of your timeline having animations polish up the entrance and exit of slide objects, leaving a smoother and more professional finish for your story.

Under the **Animations** tab, Storyline provides the **Animation Painter**, **Entrance Animations**, and **Exit Animations**. We'll talk about each of these features and how you can make them work for your story!

Entrance and Exit Animations

Entrance Animations and **Exit Animations** are animations applied to objects, which will occur when the object enters and/or exits the slide. Setting up your slide objects for entrance and exit is easy; you just have to work with the timeline to specify when you want the object to enter the slide and when you want it to exit.

In the following example, we have three rectangles: **Rectangle 1** enters at 1 second and exits at 2 seconds, **Rectangle 2** enters at 2 seconds and exits at 3 seconds, and **Rectangle 3** enters at 3 seconds and stays until the end of the timeline.

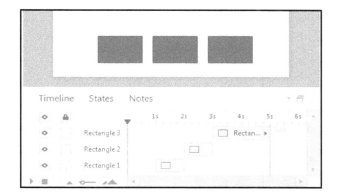

Now that the objects are where we want them on the timeline in terms of entrance and exit times, we can apply animations to them. You will do this from the **Entrance Animation** and **Exit Animation** sections of the **Animations** tab. Both are identical in terms of what you can customize.

To apply an **Entrance Animation** or **Exit Animation** , select the object you wish to apply the animation to, and then from the **Animations** tab, you will first want to select the **Animate** icon. This is where you will choose which animation style you want to use; the default is **None**. Storyline has 15 built-in animation styles: **Fade, Grow, Fly In, Float In, Split, Wipe, Shape, Wheel, Random Bars, Spin, Spin & Grow, Grow & Spin, Zoom, Swivel,** and **Bounce**.

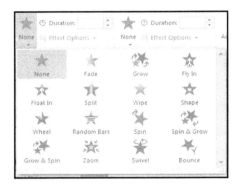

Select the animation style you want to use. In this example, we chose **Fade**. The next step will be to adjust the **Duration**. The default is **0.75** seconds. Finally, you will select the effect, which defines how you want the slide object to appear, so you can either select **None** or choose to have your slide object come in **from Bottom, Bottom-Left, Left, Top-Left, Top, Top-Right, Right,** or **Bottom-Right**.

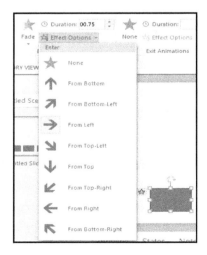

Once you have your entrance animations programmed, you can use the same methods to program your exit animations. Once all animations for the object have been programmed, you can use the **Animation Painter** to apply the same animations, if desired, to the other slide objects.

The Animation Painter

The **Animation Painter** is one of the new features in Storyline 2. It is a huge time-saver and will quickly become one of your best friends when it comes to streamlining your Storyline development. Like the **Format Painter** feature in Microsoft Office products, the **Animation Painter** will quickly copy animations from one object and apply them to others, including the animation durations and effects.

To use the animation painter, all you have to do is select the object that already has animations applied to it, then click on **Animation Painter** from the **Animation** tab, and then click on the object or objects you wish to apply that animation to.

Motion paths

Another new feature in Storyline 2 is motion path animations. If you're familiar with working in Microsoft PowerPoint, you may already be accustomed to working with motion path animations, and if you've recently made the switch from Articulate Storyline 1 to Storyline 2, you will likely become very excited about this added feature.

While entrance and exit animations allow you to move objects on and/or off the slide with no use interaction, motion path animations allow you to customize slide object movements and work in tandem with the **Move** trigger in the **Trigger Wizard**. You will notice that once you add a motion path animation, a default trigger will appear to have the animation begin when the timeline starts. Keep this in mind because you'll need to edit the trigger if you want the animation to occur in another instance.

You can create some really neat interactions with motion paths, and later on, we'll revisit the two-point toggle button we learned to create in the Exercise 1 section in `Chapter 3,` *Creating a Content-Rich Story*, to illustrate how you can create a similar effect using motion paths.

To add a motion path animation, select the object you wish to animation, and then from the **Animations** tab, select **Add Motion Path**. You'll be able to select from 10 motion path options: **Line**, **Arcs**, **Turns**, **Circle**, **Square**, **Equal Triangle**, **Trapezoid**, **Freeform**, **Scribble**, and **Curve**.

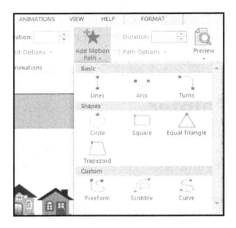

Once you've chosen the motion path you want to use, you can further customize the motion path by adjusting the animation duration and choosing relevant path options. Another important thing to know when it comes to motion paths is that there is a start point and an end point. You will need to adjust these accordingly to ensure your animation works the way you want it to work. You can adjust the start and end points by clicking and dragging to the desired location.

In the following example, we have a truck on a roadway. The goal in this interaction is to have the truck move all the way along the roadway.

The start point (**1**) is fine, but the end point (**2**) will need to be dragged further, or else it will not move for the entire duration of the roadway. Once you drag the end point, it should look as it does in the following image:

Exercise 6

Let's take a look at Exercise 6. In this exercise, you'll learn how to create the motion path effect that we just discussed:

1. On your exercise slide, you will notice that you have an image of houses along a roadway and another image of a truck.
2. To make your truck move along the roadway, you will select **Add Motion Path** from the **Animations** tab and choose **Lines**.
3. Then, you will need to change the direction of the line because the default line moves **Down**. To do so, select **Path Options** and choose **Right** because you want the truck to move from the left side of your slide to the right side of the slide.

4. You will notice that the start point is fine, but the end point does not go to the end of the road way. To move the end point, you will click on it and drag the truck to the end of the roadway or just past, extending past the slide.

5. Now when you preview your exercise slide, the truck should appear as though it is driving along the roadway. Your exercise slide should look similar to the **After** slide.

Transitions

Animations and transitions are similar concepts. Where animations focus on jazzing up slide objects, transitions focus on jazzing up transitions between slides or slide layers. Adding transitions is easy and you can apply them from **Story View** or from **Slide View**.

To add a slide transition from **Story View**, select the slide you wish to add the transition to, select the **Transitions** tab, and then choose the transition you wish to apply. Storyline has 17 built-in transitions. From this tab, you can also change the **Duration**, the **Effect Options**, or you can choose to apply the selected transition to all slides.

To add a slide transition from **Slide View**, select the **Transitions** tab and choose the transition you wish to apply to that slide.

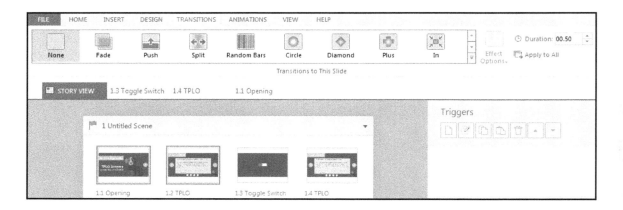

Using Zoom Region to create interactivity

The Zoom Region tool in Storyline allows you to zoom into a region of your slide, acting as a homing device for your learner's attention. This feature is great for creating interactive screenshots, conducting navigational tours, and creating hide-and-seek style interactions.

Zoom regions are timeline based; you cannot trigger a zoom region.

Adding a **Zoom Region** is simple! First, consider the area you want to zoom in on and then select **Zoom Region** from the **Insert** tab.

You will notice a green rectangle around your slide. This is your **Zoom Region**. You can move the region by dragging it and can reduce the size of the zoom region by clicking and dragging the white pull handles at the corners of the zoom region.

Zooming in on an object

In the following example, we want to zoom in on the white parked car in the image, so we'll reduce the zoom region to that area. The default transition speed is **Medium**, but you can adjust the speed by right-clicking on the zoom region, hovering the mouse over **Zoom Transition Speed**, and selecting the desired speed.

The next thing you'll want to do is move the zoom region to the desired location on your timeline. Similar to entrance and exit animations, your image will automatically zoom in when it reaches the start point of the zoom region on the timeline and will zoom out when it reaches the end point of the zoom region on the timeline.

Zooming in on multiple objects

The zoom region tool is incredibly versatile in that you can include multiple zoom regions per slide, so if you want to create a screen tour, you can easily do this by creating multiple zoom regions over the relevant screen areas and then leaving some time between each zoom region on the timeline. This will allow the slide to zoom out for a few seconds before zooming in to the next area.

You can even create a panning effect by simply inserting two zoom regions right next to each other. In the following example, the slide will zoom into the first zoom region and will then zoom in to the one beside it, effectively panning across the slide.

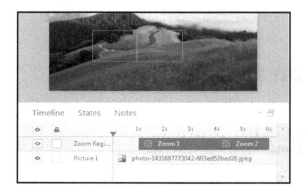

Zoom regions will always be in the same aspect ratio as the slide.

Summary

This chapter explored many ways in which you can engage your learners with interactivity in Articulate Storyline, including how to do some really neat things with buttons, markers, motion path animations, and sliders. Using these elements should keep your learners engaged with the content you're presenting and might leave them wanting more!

With all of these ways of adding interactivity to your story, you essentially learned how to help your learners become active learners, interacting with your course content and being an essential part of your story.

Now that you've learned more about triggers and have explored various elements of creativity, you should be ready to learn ways of personalizing the learning experience and creating some more advanced interactivity with variable-based interactions. In the next chapter, you'll learn all about variables and conditions that will help you take your story to the next level.

5
Using Variables, Conditions, and JavaScript

Now that you have a grasp of how you can enhance opportunities for interactivity, you are ready to take those interactive concepts and push them at warp speed ahead, creating some *next-level* Storyline interactions by applying variables, conditions, and JavaScript.

The purpose of this chapter is to show you how easily you can take your existing interactivity and bend it to your will. If you are feeling creative, you might even want to mix and match variables, conditions, and JavaScript to create a truly personalized learning experience. Applying the principles discussed throughout this chapter, you will keep your audience on their toes because they will never know what might happen next!

This chapter will show you how to leverage variables, conditions, and JavaScript to do some cool things in Storyline. You will learn how to personalize your story by creating more advanced variable-based interactions and how to implement and execute JavaScript code to add some more practical and interactive functionality to your story.

There's a lot of information in this chapter, and you might have to try things a few times to get them to work just the way you want them to, but don't worry—you'll have access to all of the downloadable Storyline files and JavaScript text documents to make development easy.

In this chapter, we will discuss the following topics:

- Overview of variables and conditions
- Using number variables
- Using true/false variables
- Using text variables
- Overview of JavaScript and its use in Storyline

- Practical uses for JavaScript in Storyline
- Fun uses for JavaScript in Storyline
- Attribution
- Summary

Overview of variables and conditions

Variables and conditions work hand in hand to allow you to easily create conditional interactivity. There are three types of variables within Storyline: text, number, and true/false variables. These variables allow you to customize the learner's experience by capturing information in one section of the story and referring to it at other points throughout the story.

 Variables and states can serve similar purposes, but the main way in which variables differ from states is that variables can be referenced at any point throughout a story, whereas states can only contain information for individual slides and cannot be referenced across slides.

We will talk more about the three types of variables next, but right now, we'll get down to the very basics.

Variables are containers for dynamic values that change based on user input or interaction. In Storyline, variables allow you to move past the basic functionality of your story into a functionally customized course. For example, you can use variables to create progress meters and track learner progress throughout the course, you can use variables to create interactive calculations, or you can use variables to mimic the style of adaptive learning paths to personalize learning.

Variables are created using the **Triggers** panel **Manage Project Variables** icon. They are also created automatically when a data entry field is placed on a slide:

When you select the **Manage Project Variables** icon, the **Variables** panel will appear. This is where you will manage all of your project variables. You can use this panel to add new variables, edit existing variables, copy and paste variables, and delete variables:

To add a new variable, follow these steps:

1. Select the **Create a New Variable** icon.
2. The **Variables** panel will appear. Here, you will name and select the type of variable you want to add.

 Naming variables is extremely important, especially in stories with many variables. Variable names should be practical. For example, if you've set up a text variable for a user to enter their e-mail, name the variable `Email`. Using a practical naming convention will allow you to easily locate variables in the **Manage Project Variables** panel.

3. Then, select the starting value for the variable.

4. Finally, click on **OK**, and you will see your newly added variable in the **Variables** panel.

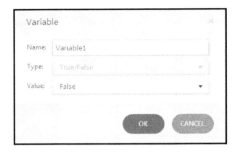

The easiest way to remember how to program a variable is to think of it as a three-step process:

1. Create: Create the variable.
2. Adjust: Adjust the variable.
3. Employ: Use the variable.

We've already talked about creating the variable, which is done using the **Manage Project Variables** panel, but we haven't yet discussed adjusting the variable or employing the variable, so here we go!

What do we mean when we say *adjust the variable*? We mean creating a trigger to incite the action you want. Once you've created the variable, you will need to create a trigger to adjust the variable appropriately. To do this, add a new trigger; you will be using the **Adjust Variable** in **Action**:

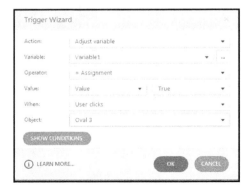

The **Adjust Variable** action provides you with some additional trigger configuration options, which, based on the preceding screenshot, are explained in the following list:

- **Variable**: This is used to specify the variable you wish to adjust.
- **Operator**: This is used to dictate whether you want the variable or value to be equal to the assignment or not equal to the assignment; in this example, we have chosen equal to assignment.
- **Value**: Here you select whether you want a value or variable to adjust, and what you want it to adjust to; in this example, our variable's default is **False**, so we want the **Value** to adjust to **True** when a certain action occurs.
- **When**: This is the same as with any other trigger; here you dictate when the variable will adjust. In this example, the variable will adjust when the user clicks.
- **Object**: This is the same as with any other trigger; here you dictate what object needs to be clicked to adjust the variable. In this example, **Oval 3** is the object.

Once you have programmed the adjust variable, you need to employ the variable!

In the example of changing the variable to **True** when the user clicks on **Oval 3**, we can use the true/false variable (**Variable1**) to prevent access to subsequent navigational elements.

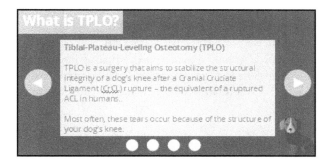

You can see in the preceding screenshot that there are four small circles below the textbox. These circles navigate from one page of text to the next. We can use the true/false variable to prevent the learner from accessing a navigational element until the previous one has been selected. To achieve this effect, you will work with the true/false variable, conditions, triggers, and states.

Keep this example in mind because we'll come back to it when we discuss true/false variables.

Using number variables

Number variables are variables comprising numeric values such as scores, clicks, or attempts. In Storyline, number variables allow you to attribute equal assignment or add, subtract, multiply, or divide values.

You can use number variables to do some neat things, such as tracking the number of times a slide object was clicked, to create conditional navigation, or to perform calculations.

Exercise 1

Let's take a look at Exercise 1. In this exercise, you'll learn how to use variables to add user-entered values. There are two slides in this exercise: a **Before** slide (slide 1) and an **After** slide (slide 2). Please note that in your **Manage Project Variables** panel, you will notice additional variables; these variables are associated with the **After** slide example and will have the prefix **AFTER**.

On your exercise slide, you will see that there are three clients, three numeric entry boxes for the user to enter values, and a **Calculate** button. Follow these steps to make this slide functional:

1. Select the **Manage Project Variables** icon. You will see that there are six variables. Ignore those with the prefix **AFTER**. The three remaining numeric variables were created when we added the numeric user-entry boxes on the slide. Each variable corresponds with a numeric user-entry box, and you can leave the starting values at 0. To simplify programming, rename each of the variables Client1, Client2, and Client3.
2. Now, add a new variable with the following parameters and click on **OK**:
   - **Name: Calculate**
   - **Type: Number**
   - **Value**: 0
3. Click on **OK** to close the **Manage Project Variables** panel.
4. Next, you will need to add triggers for each of the numeric user-entry boxes. To do this, select **Add Trigger** below the button in the **Triggers** panel and specify the following parameters in the **Trigger Wizard**:
   - **Action: Adjust variable**
   - **Variable: Calculate**
   - **Operator: + Add**
   - **Value: Variable – Client1**

- **When**: User clicks
- **Object**: Button 1

5. Then, select the trigger in the **Triggers** panel, copy and paste the trigger, and then double-click on the trigger to adjust. When adjusting, you will want to adjust the **Value** to read **Client2** and then **Client3**. You should now have three triggers below **Button 1** in the **Triggers** panel, as shown in the following screenshot:

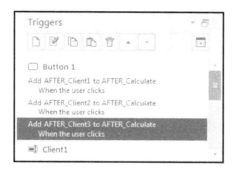

6. Finally, you need to add a variable reference. To do this, place your cursor in the textbox next to the **$** sign. Then, from the **Insert** tab, select **Reference**. You will be presented with the **Variables** panel:

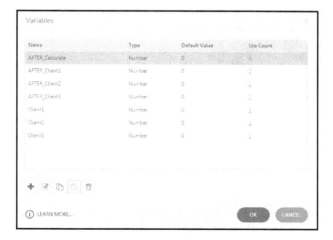

7. Click on the **Calculate** variable and click on **OK**. You will see the reference variable has appeared next to the **$** sign:

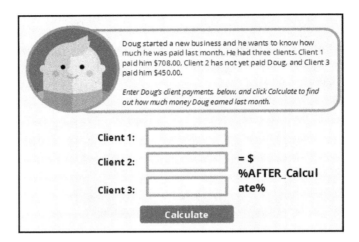

8. Now, when you preview your exercise slide, enter the values as indicated in the scenario and select the **Calculate** button; your calculation will appear. To see the correct behavior, reference the **After** slide or the following screenshot:

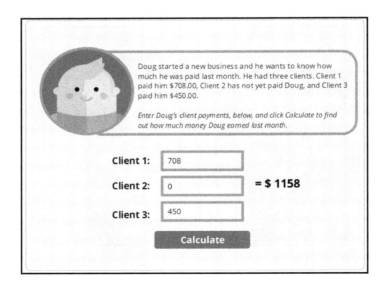

Using true/false variables

A true/false variable is a simplified boolean variable, in that it is a data type containing two values—in this case true and false. Therefore, this variable only stores two types of values: true and false.

True/false variables are a great way of creating interactivity based on opposites, for example, off/on, visited/not visited, correct/incorrect, and so on.

Exercise 2

Let's take a look at Exercise 2. In this exercise, we're going to revisit the example discussed at the beginning of this chapter. Here, you'll learn how to use true/false variables to direct user navigation. Please note that in your **Manage Project Variables** panel, you will notice additional variables; these variables are associated with the **After** example and will have the prefix **AFTER**.

1. On your **Exercise slide 1.1**, you will see that there are four circles below the slide content; these circles navigate from one layer of content to the next. The first thing you will need to do is create triggers for **Oval 4**, **Oval 5**, and **Oval 6** with the following parameters:
   - **Action: Change state of**
   - **On Object: Oval 4**
   - **To State: Disabled**
   - **When: Timeline starts**
   - **Object:** the slide

2. You should now have three of these triggers. These triggers will prevent the user from navigating to the next *pages*:

3. Next, you will need to set up three variables—one for each navigation element except for the last one (as there is no other navigation element that follows this one). So, you will set up a **True/False** variable for **Oval 3**, **Oval 4**, and **Oval 5**. To do this, open the **Manage Project Variables** panel and select **Create a new variable** with the following parameters:

   - **Name: Oval 3**
   - **Type: True/False**
   - **Value: False**

4. Do this for **Oval 3**, **Oval 4**, and **Oval 5**. Once you have all three variables created, click on **OK**:

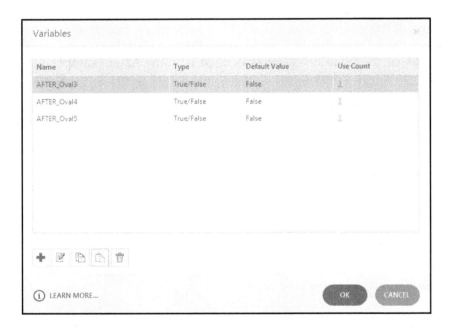

5. Once you have created all of your variables, you will need to create triggers to use the variables. You will need to create two triggers for each navigation element. First, add a new trigger with the following parameters—do this for **Oval 3**, **Oval 4**, and **Oval 5**:

   - **Action: Adjust variable**
   - **Variable: Oval 3**
   - **Operator: = Assignment**
   - **Value: Value, True**

- **When: User clicks**
- **Object: Oval 3**

6. Then, you will need to create another trigger to change the state of each navigational element from **Disabled** to **Normal**. To do this, add a new trigger and use the parameters specified in the following; do this for **Oval 4**, **Oval 5**, and **Oval 6**:
    - **Action: Change state of**
    - **On Object: Oval 4**
    - **To State: Normal**
    - **When: Variable changes**
    - **Variable: Oval 3** (the navigation element previous to the on object)

7. Select **Add a new AND** or **OR** condition, and in the **Add Trigger Condition** panel, specify the following parameters:
    - **List: Variables**
    - **If: Oval 3**
    - **Operator: = = Equal to**
    - **Type: Value**
    - **Value: True**

8. Now, when you preview your exercise slide, you should only be able to click on navigation elements if the previous element has first been selected. This prevents the user from jumping ahead in the content without having first accessed the previous content.

Using text variables

Text variables are a great way of personalizing the learner's experience. They allow users to interact with a text entry object on one slide, and that text entry may be referenced throughout the story. For example, a learner may be prompted to enter his/her name at the beginning of a course or module, and that name will be carried throughout the story, adding a personal touch and likely enhancing the overall learner's experience.

Exercise 3

Let's take a look at Exercise 3. In this exercise, you will learn how to use text variables to personalize the learner's experience. Please note that in your **Manage Project Variables** panel, you will notice additional variables; these variables are associated with the **After** example and will have the prefix **AFTER**.

In your exercise scene, you will see that there are two slides. On the first slide, you have a prompt to enter your dog's name with a text entry box. On the second slide, you have some text, and you will notice that there are underscores. You will be replacing these underscores with a variable reference. To make this scene functional, follow these steps:

1. First, you will want to access the **Manage Project Variables** panel. Here, you will notice that there are two variables: the variable for the **After** scene and another variable named **TextEntry**. Like the numeric user-entry field, adding a text entry field will automatically add an associated variable. Double-click on **TextEntry** and rename the variable, for clarity, to `DogName`, and then click on **OK**:

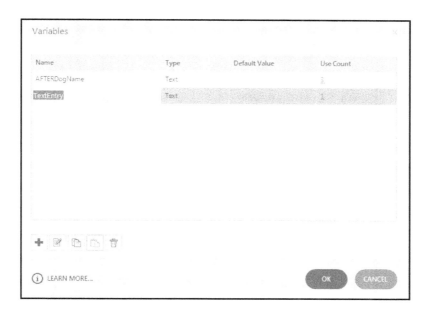

2. Then, you will want to go to slide 2, highlight the underscored area in the text box, and from the **Insert** tab, select **Reference**, select **DogName**, and click on **OK**. Do this for both sections of underscores in the text box:

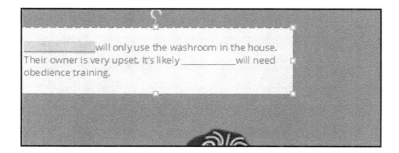

3. Now, when you preview the scene and enter a dog name on slide 1, you will see that the dog name you entered is referenced in the text box on slide 2. Refer to the **After** scene to see how the scene should behave.

Another way of using text variables is to allow learners to take their own notes throughout a course and then reference the notes at a later point. To do this, you would follow the same principles as Exercise 3—creating a text entry box where the learner will make their notes and then referencing that variable on another slide. See the following screenshots for an example of this effect:

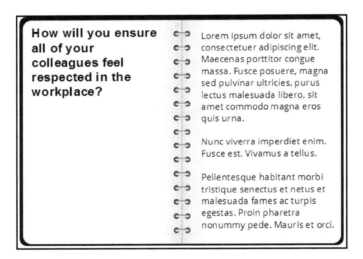

When doing this, it is often helpful to insert a scrolling panel on the slide where you are referencing the text entry. This will ensure that if the learner provided a lengthy response, the text will not scroll off the slide.

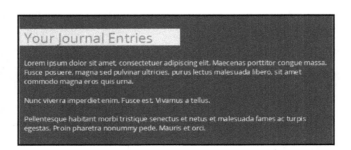

Another neat way you can use text variables is to easily create a transcript/closed captioning effect. With a few easy steps, you can use text variables to hold slide, video, or audio transcripts. Additionally, the user will be able to toggle the transcript on and off based on their individual preferences.

To achieve this effect, you will be combining the power of text variables with the power of conditions to create one super-slick effect that will make all of your students or e-learning developer colleagues drool!

Exercise 4

Let's take a look at Exercise 4. In this exercise, you will learn how to use text variables to create a transcript effect. Please note that in your **Manage Project Variables** panel, you will notice additional variables; these variables are associated with the **After** example and will have the prefix **AFTER**.

On your exercise slide, you will see that there is a slide with an avatar and some dialog. To get the transcript elements working, follow these steps:

1. Create a new layer titled `Toggle` and add a button with the text transcript to your slide above the avatar/dialog.
2. Access the **Manage Project Variables** panel and create two new variables. The parameters for the first variable are as follows:
   - **Name: Transcript**
   - **Type: Text**
   - **Value:** leave blank
3. The parameters for the second variable are as follows:
   - **Name: Toggle**
   - **Type: True/False**
   - **Value: False**

4. Now, create another layer titled `Transcript` and insert a shape below the avatar and a dialog. From the **Insert** panel, select **References**, and choose the variable you want to reference:

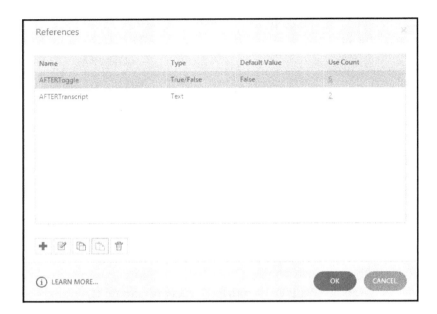

5. Next, on the **Toggle** layer, you will create three triggers. The parameters for the first trigger will be as follows:
   - **Action: Show layer**
   - **Layer: Transcript**
   - **When: Variable changes**
   - **Variable: Toggle**
   - **On Condition:**
     - **If: Toggle**
     - **Operator: = = Equal to**
     - **Type: Value**
     - **Value: True**

6. The parameters for the second trigger will be as follows:
   - **Action: Hide layer**
   - **Layer: Transcript**
   - **When: Variable changes**

- **Variable: Toggle**
- **On Condition:**
  - **If: Toggle**
  - **Operator: = = Equal to**
  - **Type: Value**
  - **Value: False**

7. And finally, you will create a trigger for the **Toggle** button you created, with the following parameters:
   - **Action: Adjust variable**
   - **Variable: Toggle**
   - **Operator: = NOT Assignment**
   - **When: User clicks**
   - **Object:** the button or shape you created

8. The **Triggers** panel for the **Toggle** layer should look like the following screenshot:

9. Now, create another layer titled **Transcript** and insert a shape below the avatar

and a dialog:

10. Then, with the shape you just created still select, select **Reference** from the **Insert** tab and choose the **Transcript** variable.

11. Next, add a trigger with the following parameters:
    - **Action: Show layer**
    - **Layer: Toggle**
    - **When: Timeline starts**
    - **Object:** the current layer

12. Finally, on the base layer, create two new triggers. The first trigger will have with the following parameters:
    - **Action: Adjust variable**
    - **Variable: Transcript**
    - **Operator: = Assignment**
    - **Value: Value**: Enter transcript text in the blank space beside the value

dropdown. In your exercise file, you will notice the sample text has been pasted in the **Notes** panel, so you can easily copy/paste to the **Value** field

- **When: Timeline starts**
- **Object:** the slide you're programming

13. The second trigger will have the following parameters:
    - **Action: Show layer**
    - **Layer: Toggle**
    - **When: Timeline starts**
    - **Object:** the current slide

14. Now, when you preview your exercise slide, you should see a transcript appear at the bottom of the slide when you click on the **Transcript** button, as illustrated in the **After** slide or the following screenshot:

15. When you select the **Transcript** button, the transcript pane will appear with the transcript text. When you select the **Transcript** button again, the transcript pane will disappear.

 For ease of explanation, we illustrated this effect on an individual slide. However, you can create this effect more easily by adding the **Transcript** and **Toggle** layers in the master slide view.

Overview of JavaScript and its use in Storyline

JavaScript is a programming language that Articulate Storyline supports by allowing the execution of JavaScript triggers. This support allows you to extend the functionality of your stories with dynamic and scripted interactions.

There are many things you can do with JavaScript in Storyline, but here we will merely scrape the surface! JavaScript can be used to generate random numbers, display messages, manipulate variables within Storyline, and generate completion certificates—and these are just a few functions!

The goal here is to provide you with all you need to know to harness your inner *JavaScriptor* and execute JavaScript in Storyline as though you've been doing it all of your life! The examples included are all practical and will be provided alongside their practical uses.

In the previous section, we discussed the concept of variables and conditions in Storyline, and you will quickly notice within this section that JavaScript and variables often go hand in hand.

All JavaScript referred to in this section will be downloadable for ease of access and use. So, if you're not keen on tediously typing JavaScript from text to the Storyline JavaScript field, we've got you covered! Just download the corresponding JavaScript text files and copy/paste the code straight from the text document into the Storyline JavaScript field.

Please note that I am in no way an expert on JavaScript, so please visit the *Attribution* section of this chapter to find out where I located some of the awesome code!

But first, some things to note when using JavaScript in Storyline:

- When using the execute JavaScript trigger in Storyline, you cannot view the JavaScript function in Storyline's **Preview** mode. You must publish the story to run the JavaScript.
- `Player.GetVar` will allow you to acquire the value of variables in Storyline, while `Player.SetVar` will set the value of a variable in Storyline.
- The maximum character length for a JavaScript trigger is 32,767.
- JavaScript triggers are not supported in the **Articulate Mobile Player** application, but they are supported in Flash and HTML5 output.

Practical uses for JavaScript in Storyline

The following sections will teach you how JavaScript works in Storyline.

Generating a word count

Word count calculators are a great way of ensuring that your learners aren't creating too much work for you when it comes to evaluating short or long answer responses. By specifying a word count, you can guide your learners to the desired length of response you expect to receive.

In Storyline, you can use variables and JavaScript to easily create a word count calculator.

Exercise 5

Let's take a look at Exercise 5. In this exercise, you will learn how to use text and number variables, in collaboration with JavaScript, to create a word count calculator. Please note that in your **Manage Project Variables** panel, you will notice additional variables; these variables are associated with the **After** example and will have the prefix **AFTER**. For ease of use, download `JavaScript1.txt` and copy/paste the script into the Storyline **Script** field.

In your exercise scene, you will see that there is a slide with an avatar, a text prompt for the learner, and a text entry box. You will also notice that beneath the text entry box, there is a button—this is our word count calculator. To get the word count calculator working, follow these steps:

1. Access the **Manage Project Variables** panel. You will notice that there is one variable already created; this was autopopulated from your text entry box. Rename this variable `Words`. Then, add a second variable with the following parameters:
   - **Name: Count**
   - **Type: Number**
   - **Value:** leave blank

2. With these two variables created, exit the **Manage Project Variables** panel by clicking on **OK**.

3. Next, you will add a trigger to the button on your exercise slide. This trigger will have the following parameters:
   - **Action: Execute JavaScript**
   - **Script:** click on the button and enter the following script:

```
var player = GetPlayer();
var content = player.GetVar("Words");
var matches = content.match(/\S+\s*/g);
var numWords = matches !== null ? matches.length : 0;
player.SetVar("Count", numWords);
```

- **When: User clicks**
- **Object:** the button

4. The script in your **Script** field should appear as shown in the following screenshot:

5. In the text field with the = sign, insert a reference to the Count variable. This is where the word count will appear:

6. Now, when you publish the story and upload it to the Web or a **Learning Management System** (**LMS**), you will see that if you enter text into the text entry box and then click on the **Word Count** button, your word count will appear beside the button. View the **After** slide (in the published and uploaded output) or the following screenshot for an example of how your slide should function:

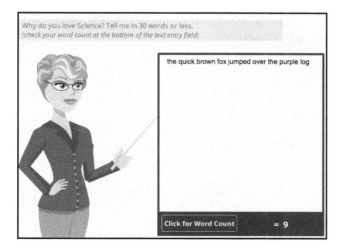

Allowing users to print the current slide

Providing learners with the ability to print from the current slide is an extremely simple and practical use of JavaScript in Storyline. When it comes to application, this function particularly comes in handy when developing stories that include journal entry or note taking functionality, when presenting job aids, and when including reference documentation.

Your first order of business when designing a slide to be printed is to include a print button or object to your slide. If you want learners to be able to print any slide in the story, you can make this easy on yourself by adding the print button or object to the master slide:

Once you have the button added, you need to make it work, and to do this, you'll add a trigger with the following parameters:

- **Action: Execute JavaScript**
- **Script:** enter the following script:

```
window.print();
```

- **When: User clicks**
- **Object:** your button or object

Your JavaScript panel should appear as it does in the following screenshot:

For ease of use, download `JavaScript2.txt` and copy/paste the script into the Storyline JavaScript field.

Generating a date

Date stamping your slides is a great way of ensuring that learners complete their training by a specified date. This is particularly beneficial in compliance-style programs, where certificates of completion must be generated or proof of completion screenshots must be taken.

With a little bit of JavaScript, Storyline easily allows you to date stamp your slides. If you want the date stamp to appear on all slides, you can streamline your development by adding this trigger and JavaScript to the master slides.

Exercise 6

Let's take a look at Exercise 6. In this exercise, you will learn how to use JavaScript to change the value of a text variable in order to generate a date or date stamp a slide. Please note that in your **Manage Project Variables** panel, you will notice additional variables; these variables are associated with the **After** example and will have the prefix **AFTER**. For ease of use, download `JavaScript3.txt` and copy/paste the script into the Storyline JavaScript field.

On your exercise slide, you will see that there is a slide with a certificate. The goal here is to add a date stamp to this certificate. To do so, follow these steps:

1. Access the **Manage Project Variables** panel and add a new variable with the following parameters:
   - **Name: Date**
   - **Type: Text**
   - **Value:** leave blank
   - Click on **OK**

2. Then, create a text box on your slide, where you want the date stamp of the certificate to appear, and with the text box still selected, select **Reference** from the **Insert** tab and choose the **Date** variable:

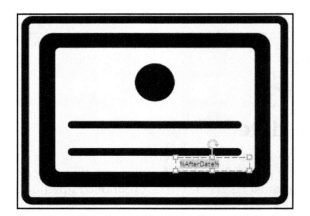

3. Now, add a new trigger with the following parameters:
   - **Action: Execute JavaScript**
   - **Script**: enter the following script:

```
var currentTime = new Date() var month =
currentTime.getMonth() + 1 var day =
currentTime.getDate()  var year =
currentTime.getFullYear() var dateString=month + "/" +
day + "/" + year var player = GetPlayer();
player.SetVar("Date",dateString);
```

- **When: Timeline starts**
- **Object:** the current slide

4. Your JavaScript field should appear as shown in the following screenshot:

5. Now, when you publish and upload your story to the Web or an **LMS**, you should see the current date on the certificate, as indicated on the **After** slide or in the following screenshot:

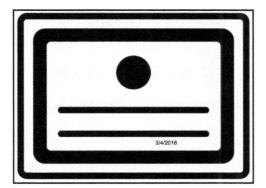

Launching and closing a timed website

Think about all of the times, as a student, you had open book quizzes, tests, exams, and so on in a traditional scholastic environment. We had a certain amount of time to complete the exam, so we had to ration the time we spent searching through textbooks for answers based on the number of questions we had to respond to within a given time.

Now, apply an e-learning lens! Using JavaScript in Storyline to launch and close a website within a certain time can allow you to create an *open book* style assessment, while limiting the amount of time the user has to review content on a certain website. And quizzing is only one type of application for this JavaScript function!

Exercise 7

Let's take a look at Exercise 7. In this exercise, you will learn how to use JavaScript to launch a website that will close when a certain time is reached. For ease of use, download `JavaScript4.txt` and copy/paste the script into the Storyline JavaScript field.

On your exercise slide, you will see a freeform question slide that consists of a prompt, a button, and three options. Here, you will add a trigger to the button to execute JavaScript to achieve the desired effect. To do so, follow these steps:

1. Select the website button and add a new trigger with the following parameters:
    - **Action: Execute JavaScript**
    - **Script**: enter the following script:

```
var myVar = setTimeout(function(){closeWin()},4000);
function closeWin()    {
                  myWindow.close();
                  clearTimeout(myVar);
                  };
```

    - **When: User clicks**
    - **Object:** the button
2. Your JavaScript should resemble the following screenshot:

3. On the second line of JavaScript code, you will see the website to be launched, and on the sixth line of JavaScript code, you will notice the value 4000, which represents the duration, in milliseconds; the window will remain open.

4. When you publish, upload, and access the output, selecting the website button should display the indicated website, as it does on the **After** slide or as illustrated in the following screenshot:

Launching a custom menu

You can easily jazz up a course by including a custom menu. This menu is programmed behind the scenes in the master slide view and is triggered using the innate **Player** menu with a little bit of JavaScript applied, providing reduced development time and a pretty neat looking effect—this one is sure to be a hit with fellow e-learning developers and clients!

To create this effect, I first added four slides to a new story: a main slide to provide orientation and navigational direction and then three content slides. To illustrate this, I formatted the background of each slide to a different color.

Once you have the slides built for your menu targets, you will want to access the master slide view. Here, you will create a new layer and add all of your menu buttons, customizing aesthetics however you prefer. You will add two triggers to each button in your menu. The first trigger will have the following parameters:

- **Action: Jump to**

- **Slide:** target slide
- **When: User clicks**
- **Object:** navigation button

And the second trigger will have the following parameters:

- **Action: Hide layer**
- **Layer: This layer**
- **When: User clicks**
- **Object:** navigation button

Your **Menu** layer should look something like the following screenshot:

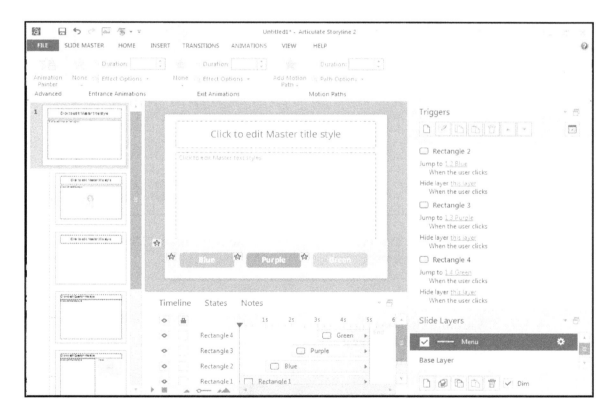

Once these triggers have been added, access the **Manage Project Variables** and add a new variable with the following parameters:

- **Name: Menu**
- **Type: Text**
- **Value: out**

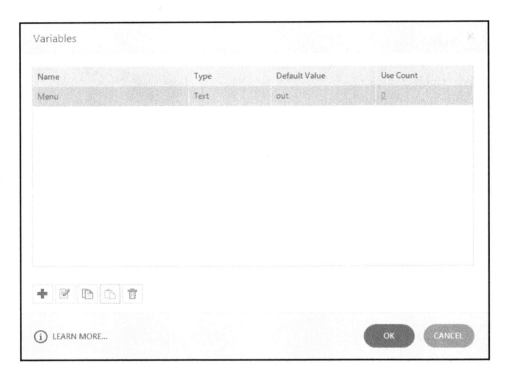

Then, on the **Base Layer** of the master slide, you will create two triggers. The first trigger will have the following parameters:

- **Action: Show layer**
- **Layer: Menu**
- **When: Variable changes**
    - **Variable: Menu**
    - **If: Menu**
    - **Operator: = = Equal to**
    - **Type: Value**
    - **Value: in**

The second trigger will have the following parameters:

- **Action: Hide layer**
- **Layer: Menu**
- **When: Variable changes**
    - **Variable: Menu**
    - **If: Menu**
    - **Operator: = = Equal to**
    - **Type: Value**
    - **Value: out**

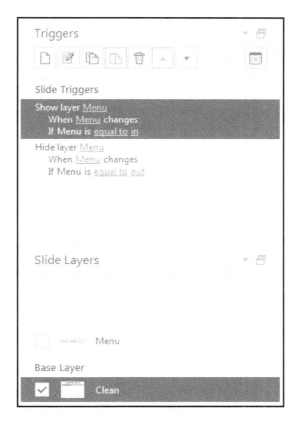

Now you can exit the master slide view and select **Player** from the **Home** tab. Under the **Player** tab, select **Add**, using the following parameters:

- **Name: Menu**
- **Align: Topbar Right**

- **Action: Execute JavaScript**
- **Script:** enter the following script:

```
var player = GetPlayer();//find the Flash Player
var Menu = player.GetVar("Menu")//get the current value or
our sl variable
if (Menu == "out") {//if the menu is out
  player.SetVar("Menu", "in")//tell the flash player to set
  the variable to 'in'
} else {
  player.SetVar("Menu", "out")//tell the flash player to set
the variable to 'out
}
```

- **When: User clicks**

Click on **OK** to close the **Player** settings, save your story, publish, and upload. Now, when you view your story online and click on **Menu**, you will see your custom menu in action! In this example, the custom menu appears as shown in the following screenshot:

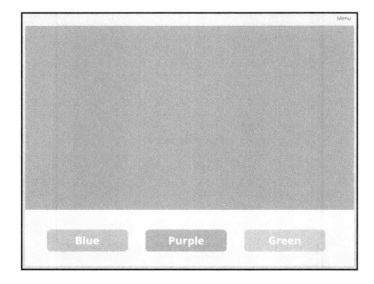

For ease of use, download `JavaScript5.txt` and copy/paste the script into the Storyline JavaScript field.

Generating a custom certificate

One of the most popular and practical uses for JavaScript in Storyline for educational purposes is to use JavaScript (and HTML) to generate a custom certificate. This certificate could be used to indicate course or module completion, or you could use it just for fun. Whatever your reason for wanting a certificate, you have covered JavaScript, Storyline, and a little bit of HTML.

This one can be finicky, so please keep an eye on your variable names within your HTML file.

Exercise 8

Let's take a look at Exercise 8. In this exercise, you will learn how to use JavaScript to generate a completion certificate. Please note that in your **Manage Project Variables** panel, you will notice additional variables; these variables are associated with the **After** example and will have the prefix **AFTER**. For ease of use, download JavaScript6.txt and copy/paste the script into the Storyline JavaScript field.

On your exercise slide, you will see a text entry field and a button. Follow these steps to make this slide functional:

1. First, access the **Manage Project Variables** panel and rename **TextEntry** to learner.
2. Select the button and add a new trigger with the following parameters:
   - **Action: Execute JavaScript**
   - **Script**: enter the following script:

   ```
   var newWin=window.open("certificate.html",
   "certificate",
   "status=0,scrollbars=0,width=600,height=480");
   ```

   - **When: User clicks**
   - **Object:** the button
3. Your JavaScript field should appear as shown in the following screenshot:

4. Next, you will want to publish your output. Download `certificate.html` and `CertBG.png`. Open `certificate.html` in Notepad and change `Afterlearner` (illustrated in the following screenshot) to `learner`, and save this document:

```
certificate - Notepad
File  Edit  Format  View  Help
k!DOCTYPE HTML><HTML><HEAD><!-- saved from url=(0014)about:internet --><TITLE>Certificate</TITLE>
<STYLE>


.result {
        position:absolute;
        left:200px;
        top:150px;
        width:360px;
        font-family:Futura, Helvetica, Arial, sans-serif;
    font-size: 26px;
        color:#000000;
        z-index:2;
}

}
.bgimage{
        position:relative;
        z-index:1;
}

</STYLE><meta http-equiv="Content-Type" content="text/html; charset=UTF-8"></HEAD><BODY><div class='bgimage'><img
src='CertBG.png'/></div>
<SCRIPT>           //this grabs the player object from the parent (launching window)      var
player=window.opener.GetPlayer();         //now we pull a field value. You can pull as many as you like. That replace
jumble lets you bring over text fields with multiple lines.       var learnerName=player.GetVar
("AfterLearner").replace(/(\r\n|\r|\n)/g, '<br />');     document.write("<div class='result'>"+learnerName
+ <br/><br/></div>");     </SCRIPT></BODY></HTML>
```

5. Then, you will want to copy both `certificate.html` and `CertBG.png` and place them both in the output folder. You will need to do this *each time* you publish. Your output folder should appear similar to the following screenshot:

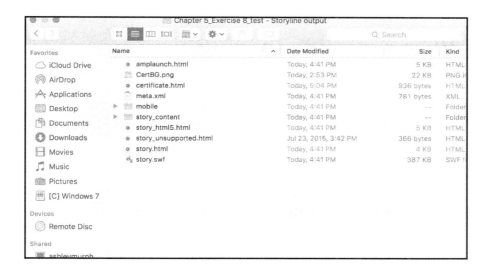

6. Now, when you upload your published output, enter a name and select the button; a certificate will be generated.

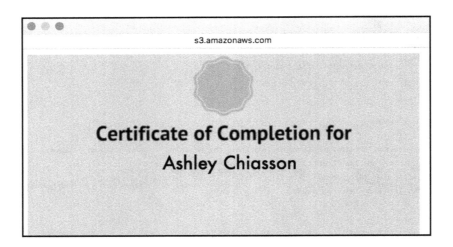

Fun uses for JavaScript in Storyline

The following sections will teach you about the fun uses of JavaScript in Storyline.

Generating a random number

Generating a random number may not be the most practical use for JavaScript in Storyline for educational purposes, but it has the potential to be useful and it's pretty easy to pull off.

For ease of use, download `JavaScript7.txt` and copy/paste the script into the Storyline JavaScript field.

To achieve this effect, you will first want to design your slide. Here, we have a text prompt for the learner and a button, which will execute the JavaScript:

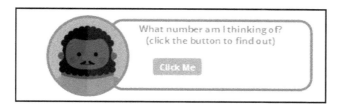

Next, access the **Manage Project Variables** panel and add a new variable with the following parameters:

- **Name: randnum**
- **Type: Number**
- **Value:**

Now that we have our variable created, we need to add a reference to the variable. This has been added next to the button:

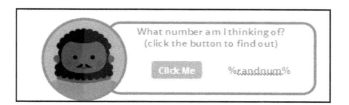

Finally, we will add a trigger to the button that will execute the JavaScript needed to generate the random number. Add a new trigger to the button with the following parameters:

- **Action: Execute JavaScript**
- **Script:** enter the following script:

```
var randomnumber = Math.floor((Math.random()*10)+1); var
player = GetPlayer();
player.SetVar("randnum",randomnumber);
```

- **When: User clicks**
- **Object:** the button

Your JavaScript field should appear as shown in the following screenshot:

Save, publish, and upload your story. Now, when you click on the button, you should see a random number generated. Note that the number will change whenever you click on the button.

Generating a pop-up alert

Generating a pop-up alert could be practical, but is seldom used in Storyline. Most alerts tend to be built out in Storyline, negating the need for JavaScript. However, JavaScript can easily generate a pop-up alert, so if you can find a use for it, this might be useful!

For ease of use, download `JavaScript8.txt` and copy/paste the script into the Storyline

JavaScript field.

To create this effect, we have first created a button on our slide. We then add a trigger to the button with the following parameters:

- **Action: Execute JavaScript**
- **Script:** enter the following script:

```
alert("HAHA! I made you click the button.");
```

- **When: User clicks**
- **Object:** the button

Now, when we upload our output and click on the button, you will see a pop-up alert, as shown in the following screenshot:

Generating a background color or image

Generating a new background color or image is unnecessary in most instances, but can certainly spice up any story. You can even get a bit more creative and have the background color or image change with each slide change (when the timeline starts), which would definitely wow (or annoy) your audience.

Creating this effect is very easy. To illustrate both effects in one example, we'll trigger the change by a click of a button. However, in a more practical application, you may wish to trigger the JavaScript to change the background color or image when the timeline starts.

For ease of use, download `JavaScript9.txt` (background color) and `JavaScript10.txt` (background image) and copy/paste the script into the Storyline JavaScript field.

For the background color, we will add a trigger to the **Change Background Color** button with the following parameters:

- **Action: Execute JavaScript**
- **Script:** enter the following script:

```
document.bgColor = "#F7941D";
```

- **When: User clicks**
- **Object:** the button

For the background image, we will add a trigger to the **Change Background Image** button with the following parameters:

- **Action: Execute JavaScript**
- **Script:** enter the following script:

```
if (document.body){
document.body.background = "BGImage.png";
}
```

- **When: User clicks**
- **Object:** the button

Publish the output, and then in the output folder, copy and paste the `BGImage.png`. You will need to do this each time you publish this file.

Now, when you upload and click on each button, one button should change the background color, as shown in the following screenshot (background changes from white to orange):

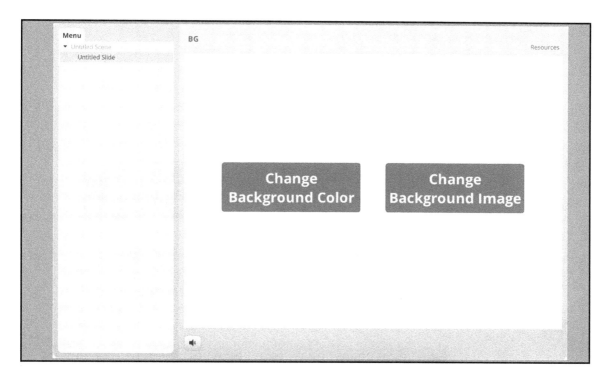

Moreover, the other button should change the background image, as shown in the following screenshot (background changes from orange to an orange floral pattern):

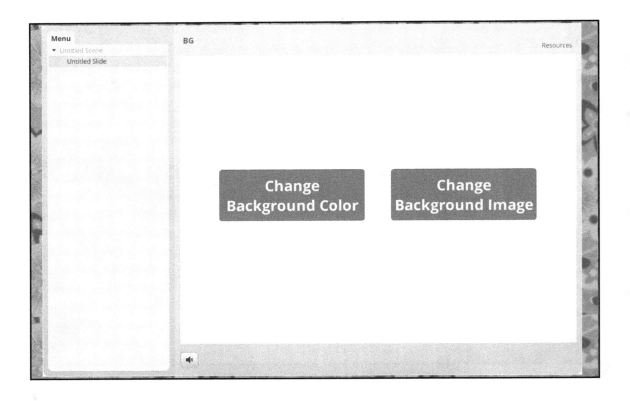

Attribution

Generate a Word Count—Phil Mayor:
https://community.articulate.com/download/storyline-2-word-count-javasc
ript

Launch and Close a Timed Website—E-Learning Heroes Community Members:
https://community.articulate.com/discussions/articulate-storyline/javas
cript-to-open-and-close-an-external-webpage

Launch a Custom Menu—James Kingsley:
https://elearningenhanced.com/blog/2012/07/03/round-tripping-variables-
storyline

Generate a Custom Certificate—Steve Flowers:
https://community.articulate.com/discussions/articulate-storyline/examp
le-files-generating-a-certificate-from-storyline

Summary

This chapter showed you how you could leverage variables, conditions, and JavaScript in Storyline to create some neat effects that step outside of the basic Storyline functions. You learned how to harness the power of text, number, and true/false variables, and how easy it is to add conditions to your variables. Then, we dove into some JavaScript uses within Storyline (practical and fun), which is often used in tandem with variables.

With all of these examples, your mind should be brimming full of ideas for how you can take your Storyline development to the next level and really deliver a customized learning experience to your audience and/or clients.

Now that you've learned how to use variables and JavaScript to bend your Storyline development to your will, you should be ready to learn all about assessing your learners and mastering the art of truly customized assessment item development in Articulate Storyline.

In the next chapter, you will learn all about assessing learning, including the assessment options available, how to master your inner convert-to-freeform sensei, how to import or export questions, how to use feedback masters to their full potential, and how to handle Storyline assessment analytics!

6
Assessing Learners

Now that you understand variables and conditions, and have some cool JavaScript exercises under your belt, you're ready to pull all of the awesome content you created together by assessing your learners. You'll probably even use some of the things you learned when you create your assessment items.

The purpose of this chapter is to show you how to create outstanding assessment items within Articulate Storyline. No more boring true/false questions—you're going to learn how to take your assessment design and development to another world. Applying design principles and interactive elements learned in previous chapters, your learners won't even mind being tested!

This chapter will focus on becoming best pals with the convert-to-freeform functionality in Storyline to create some engaging assessment items. You'll also learn how to streamline your assessment item development by leveraging feedback masters and the built-in Storyline functionality, which allows you to import/export questions. Finally, you'll get a crash course in grading and reviewing results.

In this chapter, we will cover the following topics:

- Overview of assessment options
- Using convert-to-freeform questions
- Importing questions
- Using feedback masters
- Grading and reviewing results
- Summary

Overview of assessment options

To ensure your users are actually learning (or not learning) the content, assessment options are critical, as they can show you how users are doing, and provide invaluable information when it comes to revising your content and better addressing your audience.

Articulate Storyline makes assessment easy by providing many options, which are broken out into two groups: form-based quiz questions and convert-to-freeform quiz questions.

Form-based questions are those designed by plugging information into a preset form. Convert-to-freeform questions are those designed independent of a form, or designed statically, and then converted to an interactive quiz question. Form-based questions can be modified using the options presented in **Form View**.

Storyline has 20 built-in, form-based question types. You can access the question types within the **Quizzing** tab, under the following headings: **Graded** and **Survey**. Graded quiz questions are graded using scores and have correct/incorrect/try again options. Survey quiz questions do not use scores and do not have correct/incorrect/try again options.

The built-in graded questions include the following:

- **True/False**: The user selects the correct answer from two options
- **Multiple Choice**: The user selects the correct answer from multiple options
- **Multiple Response**: The user selects the correct answer(s) from many options
- **Fill in the Blank**: The user fills in the correct term/phrase to complete the question
- **Word Bank**: The user drags the correct term to the empty box
- **Matching Drag and Drop**: The user drags items from one column to match items in another column
- **Matching Drop-Down**: The user selects items from a drop-down menu to match column items
- **Sequence Drag and Drop**: The user drags items in a list into the correct order
- **Sequence Drop-Down**: The user uses the drop-down menus to arrange items in the appropriate sequence
- **Numeric**: The user enters the correct numeric value
- **Hotspot**: The user selects the correct area within the image or screen

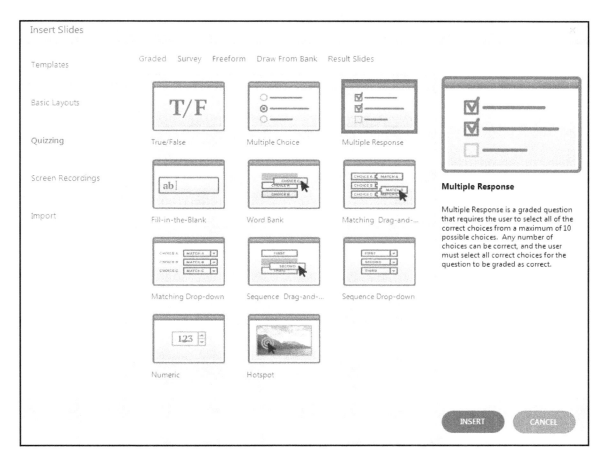

When adding a graded question, you're presented with the **Form View**, where you can define your question parameters (stem, options, and feedback) (**1**). Once you have defined your question parameters, you can specify display and scoring options (**2**). You can also see the preview of your quiz slide in the preview pane (**3**) and you can toggle between **Form View** and **Slide View** (**4**).

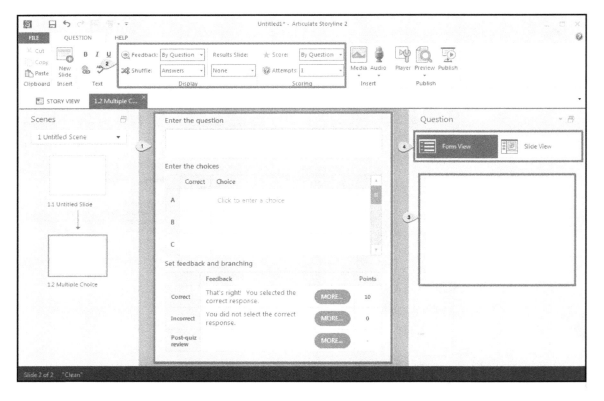

The built-in survey questions include the following:

- **Likert Scale**: The user chooses responses that best represent their own opinions
- **Pick One**: The user selects a single option
- **Pick Many**: The user chooses many options from a maximum of 10 choices
- **Which Word**: The user drags and drops the word or option that best represents their opinion
- **Short Answer**: The user may enter a short response (up to 256 characters)
- **Essay**: The user may enter a long, essaylike response (up to 5,000 characters)
- **Ranking Drag-and-Drop**: The user drags and drops options to rank them in order of user preference
- **Ranking Drop-Down**: The user selects options from drop-down menus to rank them in the user's sequential preference
- **How Many**: The user enters a numeric response

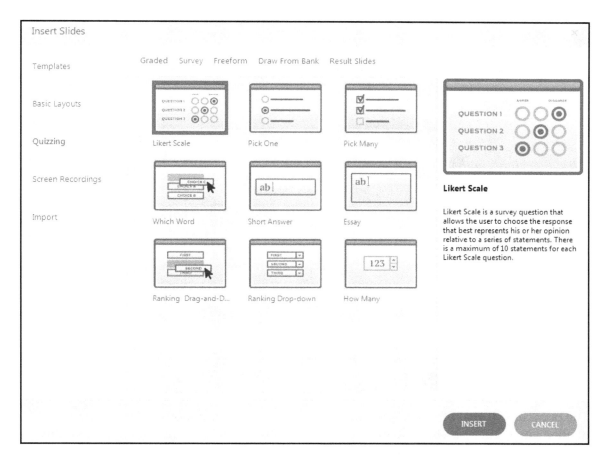

As with **Graded** questions, when you add a **Survey** question slide, you're presented with the **Form View**, where you will specify your question stem and options (**1**)—notice there are no areas to enter feedback as **Survey** questions do not employ feedback. You can then identify the display parameters (**2**)—notice there is no section for specifying scoring parameters; this is because **Survey** questions do not employ scoring. Finally, as with **Graded** questions, you can view the slide preview (**3**) and toggle between **Form View** and **Slide View** (**4**).

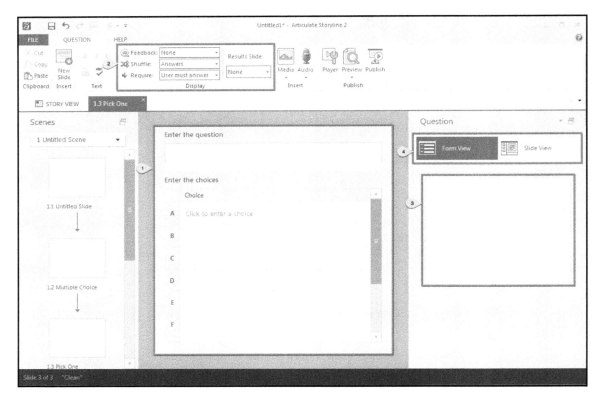

The point here is that Storyline provides you with many built-in options for creating high-quality, engaging assessment items. You can mix and match these question types, modify the look and feel of them, maintain the off-the-shelf look with Storyline's default styling ... you can do whatever you want with these questions!

But, if you're looking to create a more customized assessment item, you might want to take a look at the potential of convert-to-freeform question slides as these slides provide you with increased flexibility!

Using convert-to-freeform questions

Freeform questions allow you to take your creativity to the next level by providing a venue for creating customized assessment slides that your clients will not see anywhere else (unless, of course, you've reused these slides)! Freeform questions may be perceived as a less economical development, but they can truly help your courses stand out and may better address your course's learning needs than some of the built-in question types.

Freeform questions can take a static slide and turn it into an interactive assessment slide, and I love them because they provide me with the versatility to build out my slide first, and then convert it and program in your assessment.

With freeform questions, you have a couple of options for adding these slides:

- Add a new slide. To do so, select the **Quizzing** tab, select **Freeform**, and choose the appropriate question type
- Build out your slide. To do so, select **Convert to Freeform** from the **Insert** tab

When adding freeform questions, Storyline provides you with six options:

- **Drag and Drop**: User drags shapes or objects to defined drop targets
- **Pick One**: User selects the correct shape or object from a group of multiple shapes/objects
- **Pick Many**: User selects many correct shapes or objects from a group of multiple shapes/objects
- **Text Entry**: User enters the correct response in the text entry field
- **Hotspot**: User selects the correct hotspot(s) on a slide
- **Shortcut Key**: User enters the correct keystroke or keystroke combination on a slide

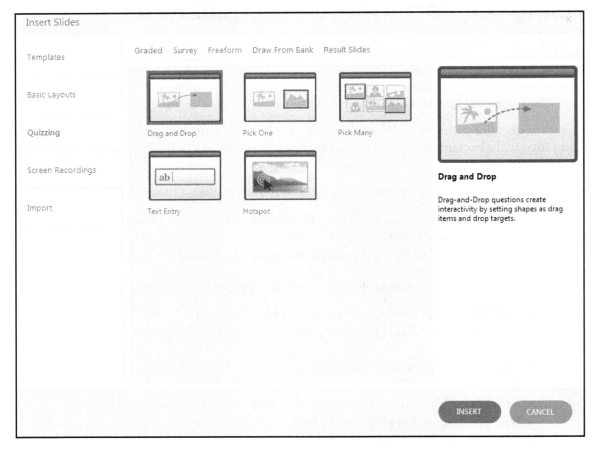

In this section, we'll go through each of these freeform slide options to illustrate just how easily you can convert boring static content into something exciting and interactive!

Drag and drop

To add a drag and drop question, you'll need to follow these four steps:

 There may be a fifth step that precedes step 1 if you decide to design the slide and then convert to freeform.

1. **Insert**: Insert the drag and drop freeform question or convert a static slide to freeform, and select **Drag and Drop**
2. **Specify**: Specify which items will be drag items and which item will be the drop target
3. **Select**: Select the **Drag and Drop** option
4. **Modify**: Modify the question properties

In the example illustrated previously, the slide has been predesigned to have a prompt, six shapes with text (the options), and an image that will be converted into our drop target.

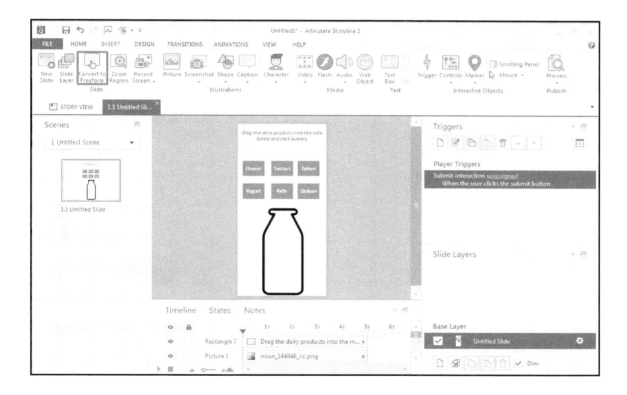

To complete step 1, you will need to select **Convert to Freeform** from the **INSERT** tab. The **Convert Slide to Freeform Question** menu will appear.

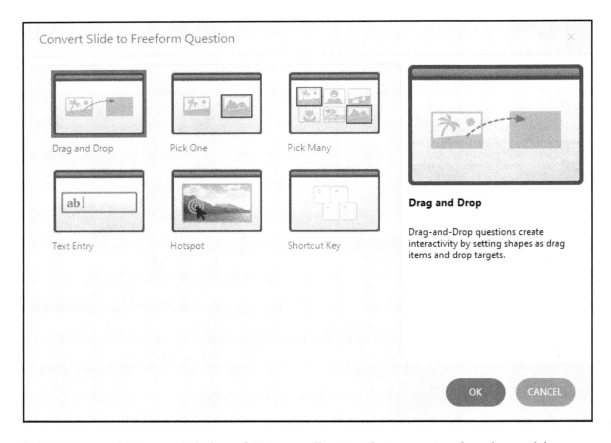

Select **Drag and Drop** and click on **OK**. You will notice that your view has changed from **Slide View** to **Form View**—don't worry! You can toggle back and forth as you wish.

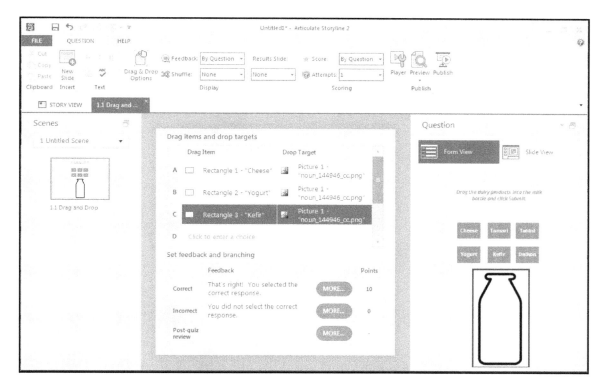

For step 2, we need to specify our drag items and drop target. In this case, the drag items are the six shapes with text. The correct response is to have **Cheese**, **Yogurt**, and **Kefir** as drag items and **Hotspot 1** as the drop target.

In this example, you can choose one of the two drop targets: you can either use the image as the drop target (shown in the preceding screenshot; the dairy bottle) or if you want to be more specific, you can create a hotspot within the dairy bottle, which is what has been done in this example (the following screenshot). The reason for doing this is that it controls the drag item positioning a bit more.

For the incorrect responses, include each **Daikon**, **Tahini**, and **Tamari** as a drag item, but with **(None)** as the drop target.

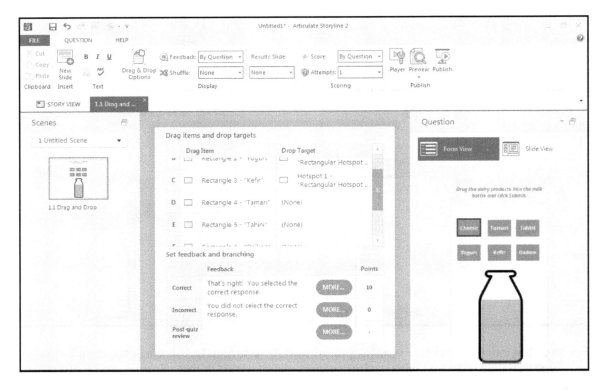

Now that we have specified the drag items and drop targets, we need to select the **Drag and Drop Options**. To do so, select **Drag & Drop Options** from the display ribbon above the **Form View**. You'll be presented with the **Drag & Drop Options**.

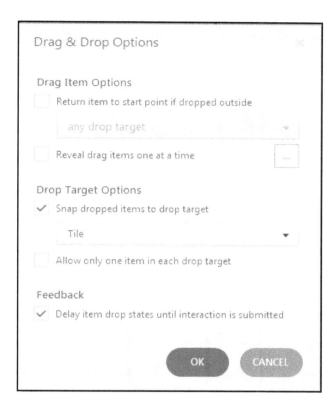

In this example, we only want to specify the **Snap dropped items to drop target** as **Tile**; this will ensure that our drag items stack on top of the next so that you can still read each of them without obstruction. The **Feedback** has been left in its default state.

Finally, you can modify the question properties. To do so, simply select the appropriate options from the drop-down menus under the **Display and Scoring** ribbons.

Now, when we preview our slide and drag **Cheese**, **Yogurt**, and **Kefir** to the milk bottle, a correct feedback will appear. Any other combination will result in an incorrect feedback.

Pick One

Pick One questions are great because you can essentially design your own look and feel for a multiple-choice question. The built-in multiple-choice question can be customized to your liking as well, but with the built-in elements, customization requires a bit more time and finagling.

Exercise 1

Let's take a look at Exercise 1. In this exercise, you'll learn how to use the convert-to-freeform functionality to convert a static slide into an interactive Pick One question type.

On your Exercise slide, you will see that there are several elements: a prompt, three shapes containing the letters **A**, **B**, and **C**, and three shapes containing the terms **Apple**, **Croissant**, and **Orange**. This is our predesigned slide. To make it an interactive Pick One question, follow these steps:

1. From the **Insert tab**, select **Convert to Freeform**.
2. Choose **Pick One** and click on **OK**.
3. In **Form View**, select each **Choice** field and choose **A**, **B**, and **C**. Then, select the radio button next to the correct choice (**B**). Your **Form View** should resemble the **Form View** of the **After** slide or the following screenshot:

4. At this point, you can modify the question properties. However, for the purpose of this interaction, they have been left in their default positions.
5. Now, when you preview the slide and select any response other than the correct response (**B**), you will receive an incorrect feedback.

Pick Many

The Pick Many question type is similar to the built-in multiple response question type, and like the Pick One question type, you can customize the slide and apply the **Pick One freeform** slide in order to allow the user to select multiple objects instead of just one.

In the previous exercise, we looked at the Pick One question type. This slide design can easily be converted into a Pick Many question by:

- Changing the question stem appropriately
- Selecting **Convert to Freeform**
- Choosing **Pick Many** and clicking on **OK**
- Selecting **A**, **B**, and **C** from the **Choice** fields
- Choosing multiple correct responses

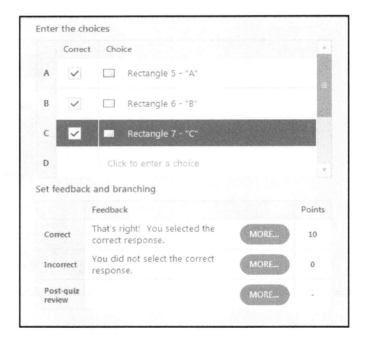

With this programming, the user will get a correct feedback when they select all three options; any other combination will illicit an incorrect feedback.

Text Entry

Text Entry freeform questions are useful for fill-in-the-blank question formats or for questions requiring a numeric response, or when either is an option.

Another advantage of the Text Entry question is that you reformat the question to place the answer field in the center of a paragraph if you wish.

Exercise 2

Let's take a look at Exercise 2. In this exercise, you'll learn how to use the convert-to-freeform functionality to convert a static slide into an interactive Text Entry question type.

On your exercise slide, you will see a background image and a question prompt. To convert this static slide into an interactive Text Entry question type, follow these steps:

1. From the **Insert tab**, select **Convert to Freeform**.
2. Choose **Text Entry** and click on **OK**.
3. **Form View** will appear.

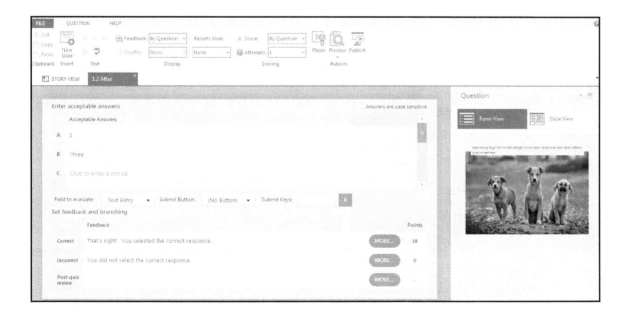

4. Under **Acceptable Answers**, enter in the acceptable correct responses; in this example, the acceptable answers are **3** and **Three**.

   - If the answers are case-sensitive, you would check the box above the acceptable answers; in this example, we do not need to check the box

5. Specify the field to evaluate and the submit button (if it's a custom button) or key (for example, if you want certain keystrokes to submit the response). In this example, the defaults are acceptable.

   - If you do have a custom submit button, select it from the **Submit button** dropdown
   - If you want certain keystrokes to submit the response (or a combination of keystrokes), enter them in to the **Submit Keys** field

Note that the *Enter* key will always submit the interaction.

6. Modify the question properties, if necessary. In this example, the default question properties are acceptable.
7. If you toggle to **Slide View**, you will notice that a text entry field has been added to the slide. This occurred automatically when you chose the **Text Entry** question type.

8. Now, when you preview the slide, you will notice that entering the acceptable answers results in a correct feedback and entering any other answer results in an incorrect feedback.

Hotspot

Hotspot question types are a great way of allowing users to select relevant areas on an image (for example, a location on a map) or to select the correct slide object.

When you convert a slide to freeform and choose Hotspot as the question type, the **Form View** you're presented with displays a preview pane on the left-hand side. This is where you can add hotspots by selecting **Add Hotspot**, choosing the appropriate hotspot shape, and drawing the hotspot on the preview pane.

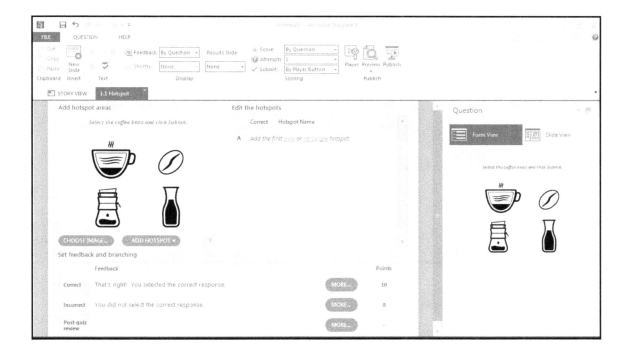

 If you begin by adding a new slide and selecting **Quizzing | Freeform**, you will likely need to choose an image. You can do so by selecting **Choose Image** and browsing for the relevant image—this method will allow you to add only one image at a time; if you wish to add multiple images at once, toggle to **Slide View**, select **Picture** from the **Insert** tab, browse for the images you wish to add, hold *Ctrl +* (select each image you wish to add), and choose **Open**.

Once you add all of the relevant hotspots, you can edit the hotspots by indicating which hotspots are correct and which are incorrect. You will see these indications in both the preview panes on the left- and right-hand sides, represented by red (incorrect) or green (correct).

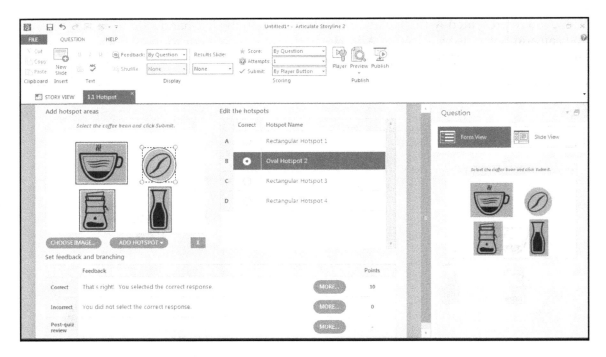

Once you have programmed all the hotspots, you can modify the **Display** and **Scoring** settings appropriately. When you preview the slide, the green hotspot will be the only one that, when selected, displays a correct feedback. Any other selection will result in an incorrect feedback.

Shortcut key

The shortcut key freeform question type allows the user to respond to a question or prompt by pressing key(s). This type of screen style may often be seen in gamified e-learning interactions, or as part of the *Try & Test* modes in screen-recorded courses, for example, having the learner respond with the arrow keys to move across a map.

Add a shortcut key freeform question by any of the following two ways:

- Designing the slide in advance, selecting **Convert to Freeform**, and choosing **Shortcut**
- Selecting **New Slide** | **Quizzing** | **Freeform** | **Shortcut**

Once added, you will be presented with the **Shortcut Key Form View**. Here, you will need to program the shortcut key question slide by selecting the **Answer** field, and pressing the keystroke (or combination of keystrokes) on your keyboard, required to submit the interaction.

 The interaction will be submitted immediately when the user enters a key combination.

As with any other question slide, you can adjust the question properties, as required.

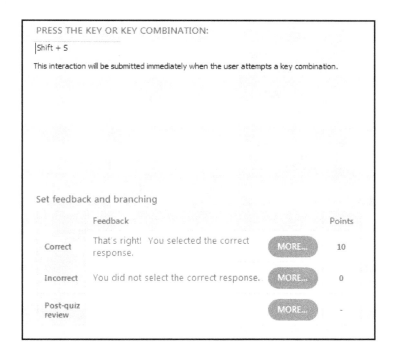

When you preview this slide, entering any shortcut key other than the key or key combination programmed in **Form View** will result in an incorrect feedback.

Importing questions

Importing and exporting quiz questions are another step in the right direction when it comes to being efficient in your development process. Storyline makes it easy for you to import questions from Articulate Quizmaker, other Storyline files, Excel, and basic text files.

To import existing quiz slides from a Storyline or Quizmaker file, select **File** | **Import** | **Quizmaker** or **Storyline** (whichever file you're importing from). At this point, you'll be presented with an **Insert Slides** menu. By default, all imported slides will be selected, but you can choose to select all or select none (**1**). Once you've selected all of the relevant slides, you can select which scene you want the slides to be imported to (**2**). Once you're ready to import, select **IMPORT** (**3**).

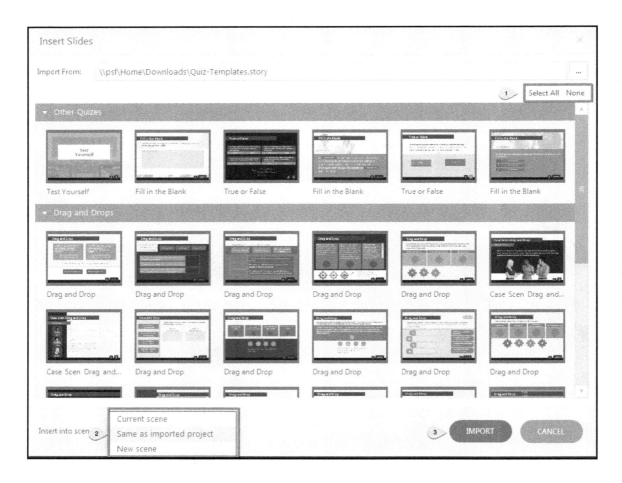

To import questions from a Microsoft Office spreadsheet, the folks at Articulate have made it incredibly easy by providing a free template.

 You can download the template from
`https://articulate-heroes.s3.amazonaws.com/import_templat`
`eeoz3qu.xls`.

Within this template, you will see the main `QUESTIONS` page and a separate page with instructions. These instructions provide all of the information you need to know in order to successfully import quiz questions into Storyline from this spreadsheet.

 If you're working on Mac OS, you will need to have Microsoft Excel installed on Windows OS in order for the import to be successful as Storyline is a Windows-based program.

Using this template, populate all of your quiz questions, as indicated in the instructions, ensuring you have populated each field. Then, save the Excel file.

Open a new or existing `.story` file, and from the **File** tab, select **Import** and then select **Questions From File**:

Once you locate and open your Excel file, the question slides will be populated in the **Insert Slides** pane. Here, you can select the questions you want to use and define which scene you want to import the questions to:

When you click on **Import**, you will see that the selected quiz questions have been imported, and all you have left to do is style the slide. Alternatively, if your story has a theme applied, the new question slides will be created in line with it.

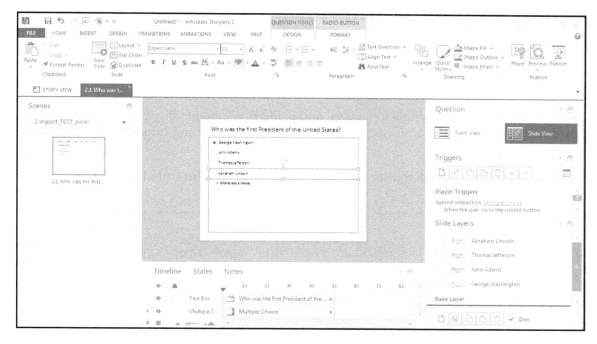

Once you locate and open your Excel file, the question slides will be populated in the **Insert Slides** pane. Here, you can select the questions you want to use and define which scene you want to import the questions to.

To import questions from a text file, Articulate comes to the rescue again with another handy downloadable template.

You can download the template from
https://articulate-heroes.s3.amazonaws.com/import_templat
eglgl1q.txt.

Once you've populated your text document, ensuring all of the applicable fields are populated, you can import the text file the same way you would import a Microsoft Excel file. As with Excel, the questions will appear in the **Insert Slides** menu, and you can select all relevant questions to import.

Using feedback masters

Feedback masters are an incredible time-saver in Storyline, and they allow you to create a custom feedback experience based on project specifications. Within the feedback master view, you can predesign your course's feedback layers by modifying the colors, fonts, text, and buttons used.

You can create multiple feedback masters, and using this functionality may take some upfront effort, but the payoff is huge when it comes to maintaining consistency throughout your course.

To navigate to the feedback master view, select **Feedback Master** from the **VIEW** tab.

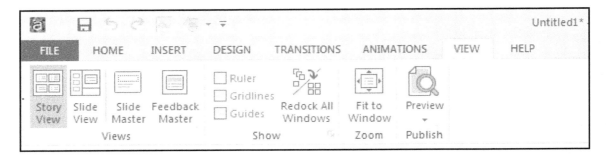

When in the feedback master view, you'll see the available feedback master—this is usually the default (as shown in the following screenshot), unless you're working on a project that has already been customized. There are two tiers to feedback masters: the master (**1**) and the layouts (**2**).

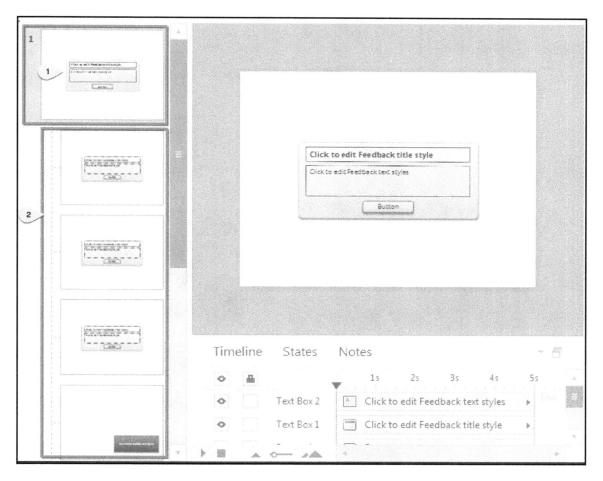

Each layout can be customized, but if you want to be super-duper efficient in developing your feedback master, you can work directly on the master slide as all layouts will automatically take on the properties of their masters.

In the following screenshot, you'll see a feedback master that has been customized. Notice that all of the layouts mimic the look of the master—the master was the only element customized and the layouts adopted this new format.

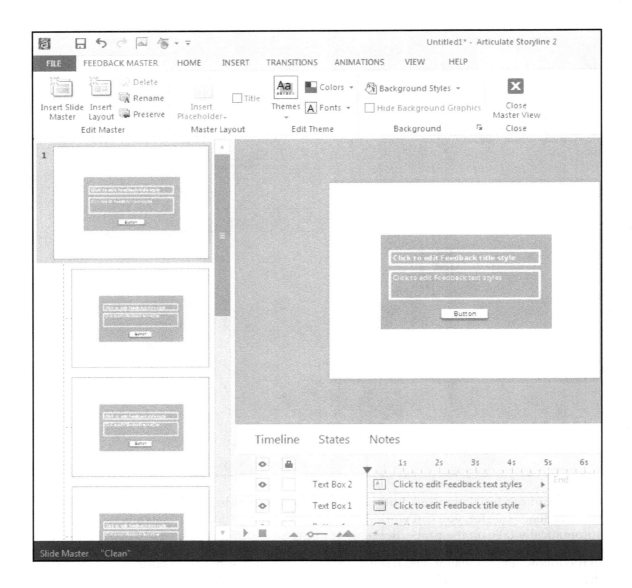

For ease of design, you can create new elements beneath the default elements, and then remove the default elements and reposition the new elements accordingly. I find this helps to ensure that feedback layer elements are maintaining a standard size as the default elements, which helps in knowing that the new elements won't spill over slide areas when you apply them in your course.

Within the **FEEDBACK MASTER** view, you have many other options, as indicated in the following list:

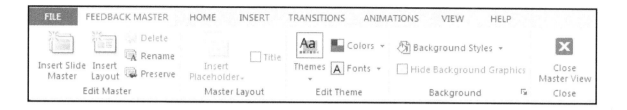

- **Insert Slide Master**: Here, you can add additional feedback masters into the same story.
- **Insert Layout**: This allows you to add layouts to each feedback master.
- **Delete**: This allows you to delete individual layouts or an entire feedback master.
- **Rename**: Here, you can name each of your feedback masters, which is helpful when planning for reuse.
- **Preserve**: This allows you to retain a feedback master that is not currently in use for later use.
- **Duplicate**: If you right-click on a feedback master or layout, you can select **Duplicate Slide Master** or **Duplicate Layout**. This functionality may save you some development time!
- **Insert Placeholder**: This allows you to insert various placeholders (for example, content, text, character, and more) into your feedback master slides.
- **Title**: If checked, a title placeholder will appear on the slide. Please note that this will only occur for feedback master layouts.
- **Themes**: This allows you to apply built-in themes or custom themes to your feedback layouts. You can also save or import themes here.
- **Color**: Here, you can specify custom or built-in color palettes. You can edit custom color palettes by right-clicking on the palette and editing accordingly.
- **Fonts**: Here you can apply built-in fonts or create a new theme font.
- **Background Styles**: This allows you to specify background styles, which you can format as you would format any slide background.
- **Hide Background Graphics**: When checked, this allows you to hide background graphics from the feedback master slide, and it only applies to layouts.

To apply a feedback layout to an existing feedback layer, select the feedback layer you want to change, right-click on the slide, select **Layout**, and choose the **Feedback Layout** you wish to apply from the provided options.

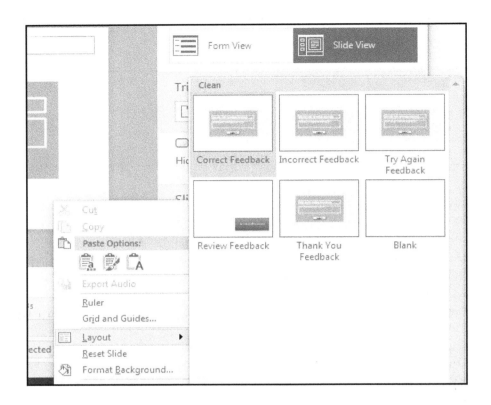

 If using the **Blank** layout, please be aware that changes made to the **Blank** layout in the feedback master will be applied to any blank slides used throughout the project (feedback or nonfeedback).

You can also achieve this by selecting the layout icon from the **Home** tab and choosing the appropriate layout, as shown in the following screenshot:

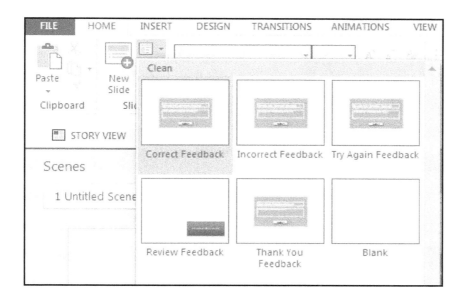

Grading and reviewing results

Now that you're armed with all of the knowledge for creating amazing assessment items, you'll probably want to actually measure how your learners are performing when they complete your beautiful quizzes.

Sometimes quiz questions are used as more of a knowledge check, where the grade is not important, but the students will benefit as a whole from responding to the questions. However, in many instances, it's critical to know whether your e-learning is effective.

This is important for a couple of reasons:

- Seeing learner results allows you to identify where learners are struggling with course content
- If your learners are not succeeding with your quizzes, it lets you know that you might have to take a different approach to ensure that learners are meeting the learning objectives of the course

The learners are not the only people getting feedback—you are too! But how do we see the results? Storyline makes this easy by providing developers with Result Slides.

Result Slides

Result Slides tend to be used to track course completion or progress in a **Learning Management System (LMS)**. They can also provide immediate feedback to the learner, on completion, of their grades or to thank learners for their participation. Additionally, **Result Slide** functionality allows users to review their responses, which may help them improve academically on future quizzes. We'll discuss the functionality in a bit, but for now, we'll go back to basics!

To add a results slide, select **New Slide** from the **Insert** tab, choose the **Quizzing** tab, and then select **Result Slides**. You have the following three options when it comes to **Result Slides**:

- **Graded Result Slide**: The user is provided with a success or failure message based on their graded score
- **Survey Result Slide**: The user will be thanked for completing the survey (or quiz)
- **Blank Result Slide**: The user will not see a **Result Slide**

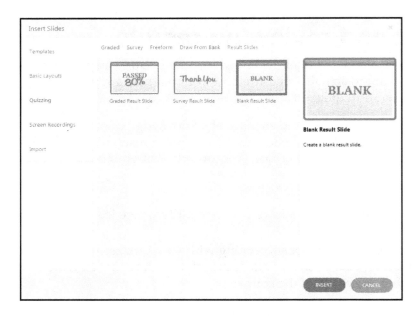

Once you select a **Result Slide** style and select **Insert**, you will see the **Result Slide Properties** appear. Here, you can choose which quiz questions will be included within the results slide. You can also indicate whether you want to calculate results for the selected questions or the selected results slides.

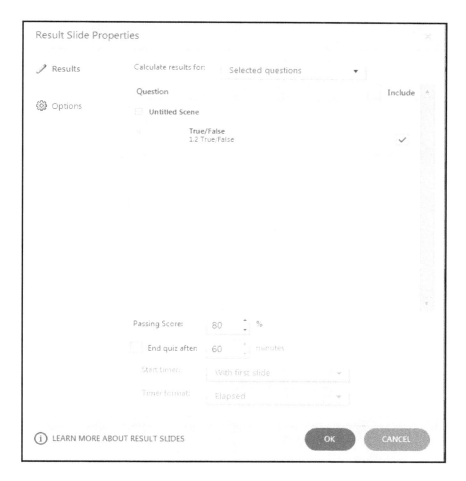

Under the **Results** tab, you also have the option of specifying the passing score, whether you want the quiz timed and, if so, for how long, when the timer will start, timer format, and so on.

Under the **Options** tab, you can customize the results slide further by indicating whether you want the results slide to show the user's score or show the passing score; whether you want to allow the user to review the quiz, and, if so, whether you want the users to be able to view incorrect/correct responses; whether you want the user to be able to print the results, and whether you want to allow the user to retake the quiz.

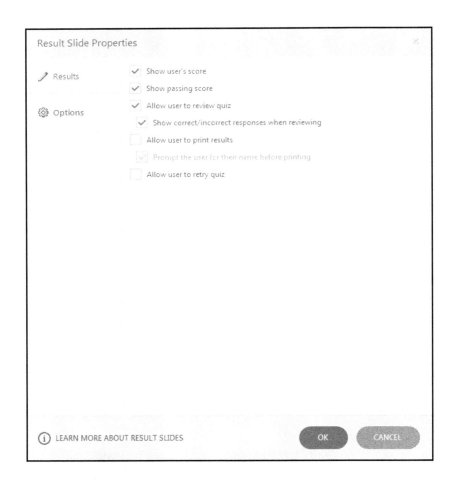

 The default selections under the **Options** tab will change based on which results slide style you choose.

Once you've customized your **Result Slide**, you can always access the **Result Slide Properties** by selecting the **Edit Result Slide** button on the **Question** panel.

When you add a graded results slide, you have the added option of customizing the success or failure messages by editing the **Success** or **Failure** layers of the **Result Slide**.

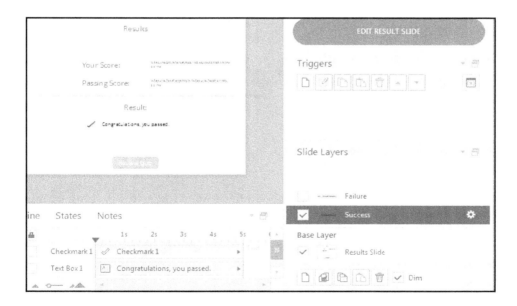

If you will be uploading your Storyline file to an LMS, you will need to tell your file to report results to the LMS. This is done when you're ready to publish. At that point, you'll select **PUBLISH** from the **Home** tab and choose the **LMS** tab.

Under the **Output Options**, you'll want to select the **Reporting and Tracking** button. The **Reporting and Tracking Options** will appear. Under the **Reporting** tab, you can identify course information and under **LMS Reporting**, you can indicate how you want the results slide to report (from Passed/Failed, Passed/Incomplete, Complete/Incomplete, and Complete/Failed)—check with your LMS provider as some LMS require a specific option and others allow you to choose. Under the **Tracking** tab, you can identify whether you want to track progress based on number of slides viewed or whether you want to track using quiz result.

When you select **Track using quiz result**, you must choose the **Result Slide** to report, so here we come back to the concept of results slides, and this is where you will identify the **Result Slide** you wish to report. Once learners begin completing quizzes, you will see their results, as you specified, in the LMS.

Summary

This chapter showed you how easily you could create customized quizzes to suit most all of your assessment needs. Storyline truly makes assessing your learners an easy process. With all of the built-in functionality, coupled with the power of the convert-to-freeform function, you will not be at a loss for assessment options.

With all of these examples, your mind should be brimming full of ideas for how you can take your Storyline development to the next level and really deliver a customized learning experience to your audience and/or clients.

You should now be able to let your controlling tendencies take over by harnessing the power of feedback masters, which allow you to provide consistency in your courses, and you should feel comfortable programming results slides for optimal student progressing reporting.

In the next chapter, you will learn all about customizing the course player, including how to organize and edit player tabs, how to customize navigation and manage the story menu, how to change the color scheme, how to add and manage resources or glossaries, how to customize player properties, and how to finally publish the story you've been slaving over!

7
Preparing to Publish Your Story

Now that you've become best buds with the convert-to-freeform tool, and have mastered the art of harnessing your inner assessor using Articulate Storyline's built-in and custom assessment options, you're ready to learn how to customize your player and publish your Story to be shared with your audience.

The purpose of this chapter is to show you how easily you can leverage Storyline's player customization options to create a unique look and feel that will address each of your project's needs. You can take the route of keeping the player as it is (there's nothing wrong with that) or you can take things one step further and create or align your Storyline player with your personal, corporate, or institutional branding standards.

This chapter will focus on taking you through each of the player customization options, explaining how to modify and/or manage them and how to choose the publishing option that will work best for your needs. We'll move from basic concepts, such as managing your Story's menu, to more complex topics, such as changing the player color scheme or publishing your Story to external sites such as Dropbox.

In this chapter, we will discuss the following topics:

- Customizing the player
- Publishing your Story

Customizing the player

The course player is the overall interface for your Story. It's the frame around your slides and it usually looks something like the following:

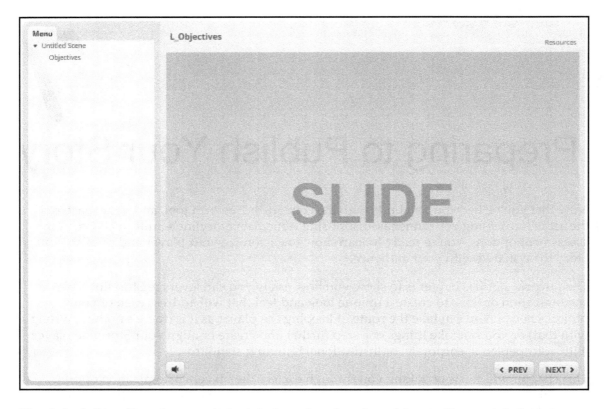

The default Storyline player gets the job done, but there's nothing really special about it, right? Well, powered by your own creativity, you can convert the downright default into something simply spectacular, and this chapter is going to guide you along this customization journey! But first, we need to cover our basics and do a little bit of an overview.

To access the **Player Properties** panel, select **Player** from the **HOME** tab or select the **Player** button in **Story View**, as shown in the following screenshot:

You'll be presented with the **Player Properties** panel, as shown in the following screenshot:

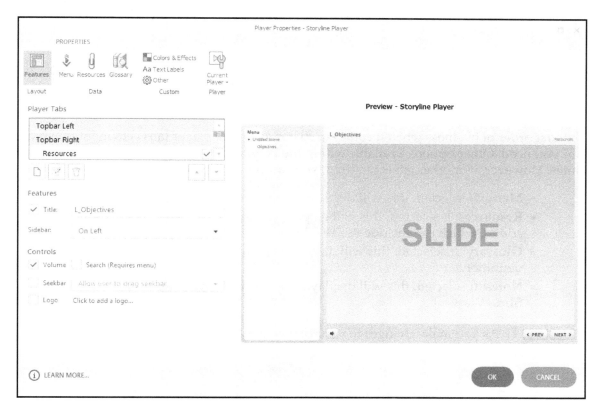

Within the **Player Properties** panel, you can do so many things. There's a lot of information to cover, so let's get to it!

 Whenever you make changes to the **Player**, you should save your changes by selecting **Current Player** from the **Player Properties** panel and then selecting **Save**.

Customizing player tabs

Within the **Player Properties** panel, under the **Features** tab, there is a section on the left-hand side dedicated to the **Player Tabs**. By default, the **Resources** and **Menu** tabs are selected. The default positions of these tabs are: **Resources: Topbar Right**, and **Menu: Sidebar**.

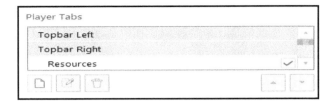

The first order of business when it comes to customizing the player tabs is to identify which tabs you need. Other options available within the **Player Tabs** list include **Glossary** and **Notes**. However, if another tab is required, you can always add it:

- **Menu**: If selected, this will display a menu for your Story
- **Resources**: If selected, this will display an area that allows extra information to be added, which can include file attachments and web links
- **Glossary**: If selected, this will display an area containing glossary terms and definitions
- **Notes**: If selected, this will display an area containing notes from the **Notes** tab in **Slide View**

 As you make changes to your player tabs, you can see the changes in the **Player Preview** on the right-hand side.

If you decide that you don't want any player tabs, just deselect all options, and your player tabs will be removed.

You can also reposition player tabs. For example, if you want a menu, but you don't want the bulk of a menu on the **Sidebar**, you can move the menu.

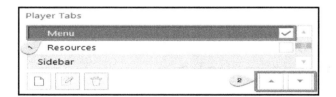

To do this, select **Menu** (1), and using the up and down arrows (2), move the menu to the **Topbar Left** or **Topbar Right**. Repositioning the menu to the topbar will create a drop-down style tab. Now, instead of having a bulky sidebar menu, your users can select **Menu** to reveal the dropdown.

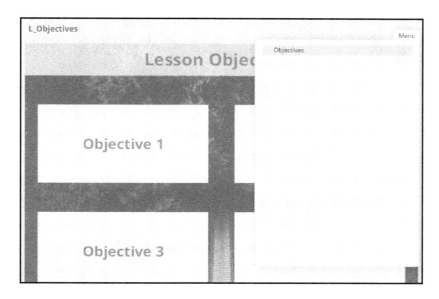

You can reposition any of the player tabs using the up and down arrows.

If there is a **Player Tab** you need, but don't see in the default options, you can add a new one. To do this, select the add icon.

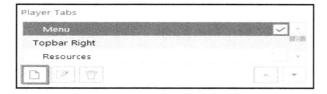

A **Trigger Wizard** will appear, as shown in the following screenshot:

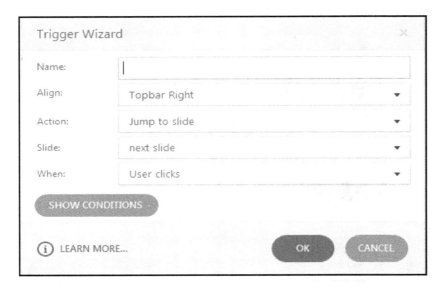

Here, you will need to define the following options:

- **Name**: The name of your player tab.
- **Align**: Where you want the player tab to appear.

 You can only show four built-in player tab options (**Menu**, **Resources**, **Glossary**, and **Notes**) in the sidebar. If you add new tabs, they can only be placed in the topbar.

- **Action**: What you want the player tab to do on selection.
    - The default is **Jump to slide**, but you have several other options (shown in the following screenshot). I've often created an instructions tab that, when selected, shows a **Lightbox slide** with navigation instructions, or an **Exit course** tab that, when selected, exits the course.

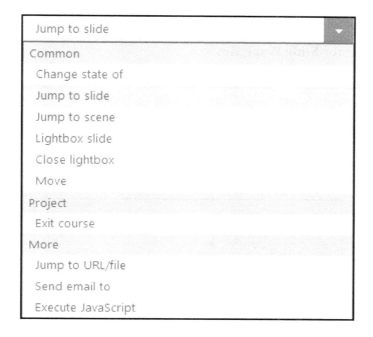

- Depending on which action you select, as with any trigger, the next drop-down menu will change (for example, **Jump to slide** shows slide as the next dropdown).
- **When**: When you want the action to occur.

Once you click on **OK**, you will see the tab that you created in the position you defined on your player preview, and it will appear in the player tabs menu, where you can edit, reposition, or delete the tab.

 If you don't want to permanently delete a created player tab, but you don't want it shown on your player, simply uncheck the box beside the associated tab. Otherwise, selecting the trash can icon will delete the player tab permanently, and if you need that tab later on, you will need to add it again.

Once you have identified which player tabs your project requires and have programmed them in the **Player Properties** panel, you still have the option to adjust player tabs on a slide-by-slide basis. This allows you to create a customized user experience, while maintaining project-specific tabs. Think of programming player tabs in the **Player Properties** panel as working with a hypothetical player tabs master.

To adjust player tabs on a slide-by-slide basis, exit the **Player Properties** panel and navigate to a slide (in Story or Slide View, it doesn't matter which).

In **Slide View**, select the **Slide Properties** icon.

The **Slide Properties** panel will appear.

From the **Player Features** drop-down menu, select **Custom for selected slides**. Your player tab options will appear. Here, you can check or uncheck player tab options and they will appear or not appear on the selected slides, respectively.

In **Story View**, you can edit the player tabs for a slide by selecting the slide, then on the right-hand side, in the **Slide Properties** panel, select **Custom for the selected slides** from the **Player features** drop-down menu, and then check or uncheck player tab options.

You cannot deselect custom player tabs from the **Player features** dropdown menu; they must be deselected in slide view.

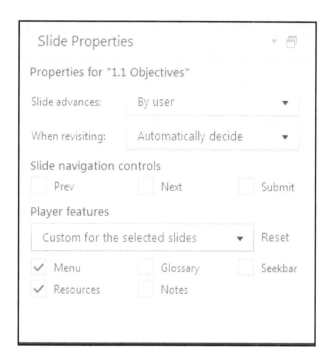

Selecting player controls and adding logos

Below the player tabs in the **Player Properties** panel, you'll see the following two sections:

- **Features**
- **Controls**

The following two elements are in the **Features** section:

- **Title**: This is selected by default. Here, you can identify a course title, which will appear in the top-right of the player, or you can uncheck **Title**, and no title will appear.
- **Sidebar**: Here, you can define where you want the sidebar to appear, **on Left** or **on Right**. By default, the sidebar is set to appear **on Left**.

The **Controls** section allows you to customize the player controls and add a logo to your player.

- **Volume**: This control is selected by default. Selecting this control provides your player with a volume icon for which the user can toggle slide volume on or off.
- **Search**: When this is selected, a search field will appear in the menu (which also needs to be selected).
- **Seekbar**: This control allows users to see where they are in a slide (with regard to the slide timeline). A pause, play, and replay icon will be included with the seekbar.
- **Logo**: This control allows you to include a logo or branding in your player. This will appear in the sidebar.
    - To add a logo, select the checkbox beside **Logo**, click on **Click to add logo...**, and browse for the desired image.

With all player controls selected, your player will look similar to the following screenshot:

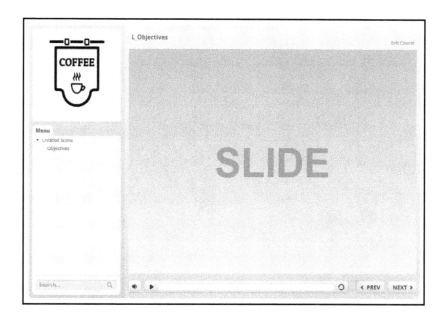

Exercise 1

Each of the exercises in this chapter will build upon the concepts discussed throughout the chapter. Let's take a look at Exercise 1. In this exercise, you'll make modifications to the **Player Properties** panel:

1. In your Exercise 1, access the **Player Properties** panel.
2. Then, disable all of the checked functions.
3. When you are finished disabling checked functions, your player preview should look like the following screenshot:

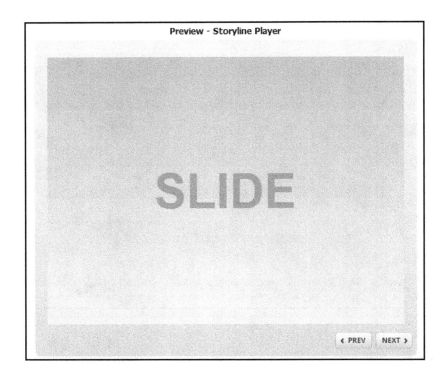

4. Once you're satisfied with the appearance of your course player, select **OK**.

This wasn't an advanced exercise by any stretch, but as we proceed through this chapter, you will build upon the preceding concepts with new modifications.

Managing your Story's menu

The menu in Storyline is great because it compiles your scene and slide names and puts them together automatically. Very neat. Way better than manually creating a menu, am I right?

To access the **Menu** properties panel, select **Menu** from the **PROPERTIES** panel, as shown in the following screenshot:

You'll be presented with the **Menu** properties panel, as shown in the following screenshot:

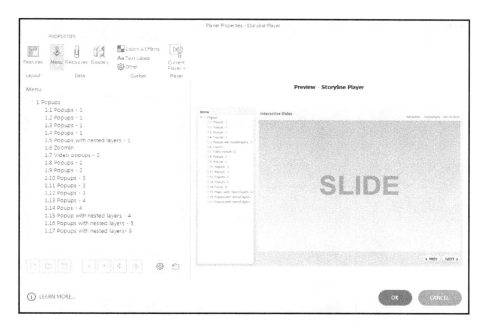

Here, you can customize the menu by adding/deleting headings, adding menu items from the project, moving menu items up or down in the menu, and promoting or demoting menu items. You can also modify the menu options or reset the menu to the default settings.

Changing a slide or scene title

One of the easiest things to do when customizing your menu is to change the slide or scene title. To do this, simply double-click on the scene or slide name you wish to change and enter the new name.

Scene or slide names changed in the **Menu** properties panel will remain unchanged in the Story or slide view.

You can avoid having to change slide or scene names in the **Menu** properties panel by changing these names in Story or slide view.

Adding and deleting menu items

Adding menu items is incredibly easy. All you have to do is select **Insert** from project icon (the folder), and from the **Insert Menu Item** panel, select the menu items you wish to add and click on **INSERT**.

You may wish to rearrange your menu items after inserting additional menu items if slides now appear out of order, so keep an eye on that.

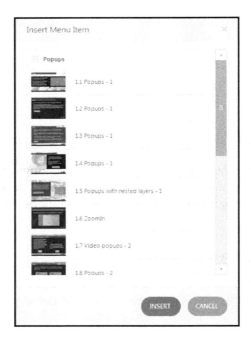

To delete menu items, simply select the menu item you wish to delete and click on the delete icon (the trash can).

Rearranging menu items

You can easily rearrange menu items by using the Up/Down and Promote/Demote buttons. To do so, simply select the scene or slide you wish to rearrange, and select the appropriate button.

Using the Promote/Demote buttons can easily tier menu items and works great to indicate main and sub-topics.

You can only demote menu items to one level further than the menu item above it. When published, promoted items will have a collapsed triangle beside the menu item. When selected, the menu items demoted below the original menu item will appear.

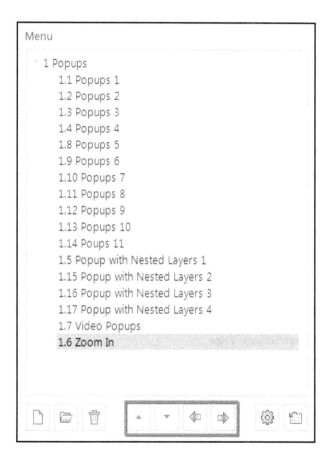

Additional menu options

So, you've modified your menu, but something's missing… you're looking for more options. Well, you're in luck. Storyline has got you covered with a few more options for customizing the player menu.

To access these additional options, select the additional options icon.

The **Menu Options** panel will appear, as shown in the following screenshot:

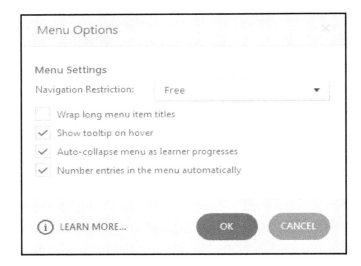

Within the **Menu Options** panel, the following items are selected by default:

- **Navigation Restriction: Free**
- **Show tooltip on hover**
- **Auto-collapse menu as learner progresses**
- **Number entries in the menu automatically**

However, you can configure your menu to suit your project. Here is what each of the menu options means:

- **Navigation Restriction**: This option dictates how the user can navigate the course.
    - **Free**: The user can navigate using the menu, moving from one slide to another and back in any order they wish.
    - **Restricted**: The user can view the current slide and any of those they've already viewed; however, they cannot view slides they have not yet visited.
    - **Locked**: The user can only move through slides in the order they've been programmed.

Many courses developed with 508 compliance in mind, or those whose content is required knowledge, often have locked navigation.

- **Wrap long menu item titles**: If you have long scene or slide names, selecting this option will wrap the long menu item titles.
- **Show tooltip on hover**: If you have long scene or slide names, and have chosen not to wrap the long menu item titles, selecting this option will show the full scene or slide name when the user hovers over the title in the menu.
- **Auto-collapse menu as learner progresses**: With this option selected, the menu items containing submenu items will automatically collapse as the learner moves past each menu item.
- **Number entries in menu automatically**: With this option selected, menu items will be numbered automatically. With this option deselected, the numbers will be removed from menu items.

Resetting menu items

Finally, say you've made changes to the menu items (for example, changing scene or slide names), and you decide after doing this that you no longer want to save your menu item changes—don't worry!

You can easily reset your menu items by selecting reset from Story icon. Doing this will reset all changed scene or slide titles to the original scene or slide names from your Story.

Adding and managing resources

The Storyline player provides the option for developers to include additional resources within their stories. These resources can be very helpful as they can reduce the amount of time learners spend on other materials outside of the LMS, which is important for security purposes, and it can provide learners with a bank of additional information to support their learning.

 If you want your learners to be able to access the **Resources**, ensure you have **Resources** selected in the player tabs section.

Adding resources is very simple. First, select **Resources** from the **PROPERTIES** panel, as shown in the following screenshot:

The **Resources** panel is very straightforward.

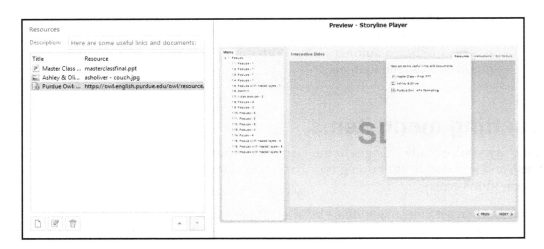

There are only five elements:

- **Description**: By default, this will read **Here are some useful links and documents:** but you can change it to whatever you want.

- **Add Icon**: This icon allows you to add new resources. When selected, the **Add Resource** panel will appear, and you can add URLs or files and change the titles accordingly.

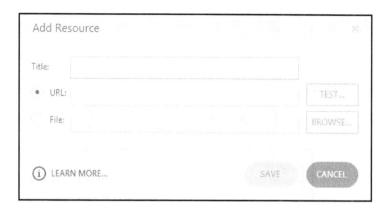

- **Edit Icon**: This icon allows you to edit a selected resource (for example, editing the title, URL, or file).
- **Delete Icon**: This icon allows you to delete a selected resource.
- **Up/Down Arrows**: The up/down arrows allow you to move a selected resource up or down in the resource list.

 When you make changes to the **Resources**, you can see the changes in the **Preview** panel on the right-hand side.

Adding and managing a glossary

Glossaries can be critical, especially in courses that are laden with acronyms or terms that may be unfamiliar to the user. As with Resources, Storyline makes adding a glossary incredibly easy.

 If you wish to include a glossary in your Story, ensure you have **Glossary** selected in the player tabs panel.

To access the **Glossary** panel, select **Glossary** from the **PROPERTIES** panel, as shown in the following screenshot:

The **Glossary** panel is even more straightforward than the **Resources** panel.

The **Glossary** panel comprises only four elements:

- **Glossary**: Here you will see all of the glossary items that have been added.
- **Add Icon**: This icon allows you to add a new glossary term. When selected, you are presented with the **Glossary Term** panel. Here, you will identify the glossary term and then provide the definition.
- **Edit Icon**: This icon allows you to edit the selected glossary term.

- **Delete Icon**: This icon allows you to delete the selected glossary term.

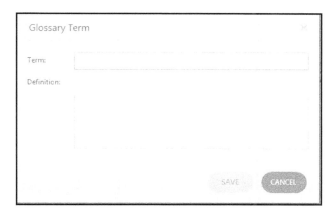

Changing the color scheme

One of my favorite features in the Storyline is **Colors & Effects**. This feature is my favorite because it allows you to truly customize the player appearance. Storyline provides 10 built-in color schemes, but the best part of this feature, in my opinion, is the advanced color editing options. The options are endless!

To access the **Colors & Effects** panel, select **Colors & Effects** from the **PROPERTIES** panel, as shown in the following screenshot:

The **Colors & Effects** panel will appear. Here, you can change the color scheme of the player using built-in schemes, or by building your own in the advanced color editor you can change the page background color, the player font, and the player text size (you can make the player text up to 200 percent larger).

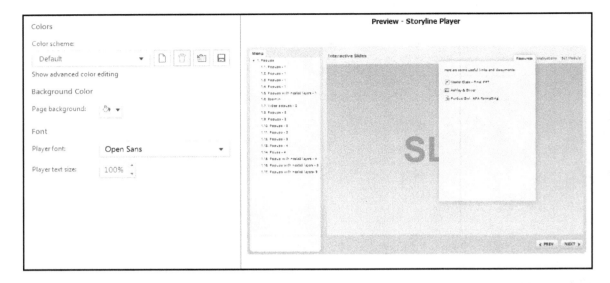

Beginning with the **Colors** section, you can change the color scheme to a built-in scheme by choosing the desired scheme from the **Color scheme** drop-down menu.

Here you can also create a new custom color scheme by selecting a color scheme to begin with, and then selecting the duplicate selected color scheme icon.

Once duplicated and renamed, you can access the color editor by selecting **Show advanced color editing**.

Within **Hide advanced color editing**, you can customize every single element of the player, choosing colors that best suit your project. Once you have your custom color scheme defined, you can save the color scheme to file, reset the Story's originally selected color scheme, or delete the color scheme.

 David Fair created a very helpful Storyline player breakdown job aid. You can access it at `https://community.articulate.com/download/stor yline-2-player-colors`.

Using the eyedropper tool when creating a new color scheme can truly set your projects apart from other Storyline projects, in that you can customize the player colors to exact branding guidelines, extending past the standard theme colors provided by most authoring programs.

Next, you may wish to change the background page color. This will change the background color of the web page the player sits against; the default color is white.

 When you change the **Page background** color (**1**), you will see the change in the player **Preview** pane (**2**).

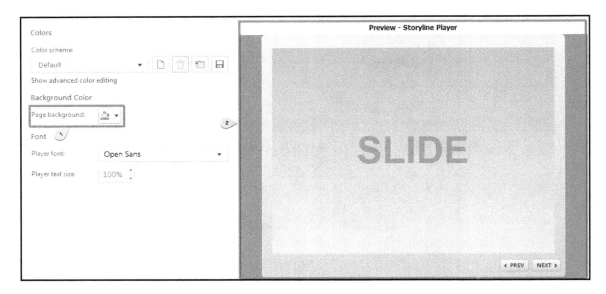

Finally, within the **Font** section, you can change the player font to any installed font and you can increase or decrease the player text size according to the needs of your project.

Exercise 2

Each of the exercises in this chapter will build upon the concepts discussed throughout this chapter. Let's take a look at Exercise 2. In this exercise, you'll learn how to do some basic customization of the color scheme of your player:

1. In your Exercise 2, access the **Player Properties** panel.
2. Select **Colors & Effects**.
3. Select duplicate the selected color scheme and title this scheme `Custom_Color`.
4. Select **Show advanced color editing**. For the purpose of this example, we will only make several small adjustments.
5. Select the edit item drop-down menu, hover over base, and select main border.
6. Drag your **Player Properties** panel to the side so that you can see some of your slides in slide or Story view, and then choose the **Top color** drop-down menu and select the eyedropper. Use the eyedropper to select the dark green color from one of your slides. Do the same with the **Bottom color**.

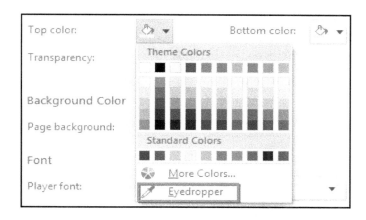

7. From the edit item drop-down menu, hover over base, and select main background.
8. Finally, choose white as the **Top color** and as the **Bottom color**.
9. Click on save icon beside the **Color scheme** menu. This will save your `Custom_Color` scheme, then click on **OK** to save and close the **Player Properties** panel.
10. When your preview your project, your player should look similar to *Exercise 2_After* or to the following screenshot—a much more modern look than the default player colors!

Customizing text labels

Another neat thing that Storyline lets you do is change text labels for all onscreen messages—there are 125 of them, so this is really neat.

To make changes to the text labels, you'll need to access **Text Labels** from the **PROPERTIES** panel.

The **Player Text Labels** panel will appear, as shown in the following screenshot:

Here you can do several things. If your project is in a language other than English, you can change the language of all 125 text labels in one fell swoop by choosing one of the built-in languages or by importing a new language file (which will be an XML file).

Alternatively, you can change individual text labels. One that I change often is the notes label to read transcript. To do this, simply scroll down until you find **Notes** tab under the **Buttons/Messages** column (they are in alphabetical order), double-click on **Notes** in the **Custom Text** column, highlight the text, and replace it with **Transcript**. It's just that simple, and you can do this for any of the buttons/messages, including the default correct/incorrect feedback.

When you're finished updating the text labels, click on **Update Preview** to see your changes in the **Preview** pane.

Additional customization

As if all of that customization wasn't enough, Storyline provides you with several final options for customizing your course player. You can access these options by selecting **Other** from the **PROPERTIES** panel, as shown in the following screenshot:

The **Browser Settings** panel will appear, as shown in the following screenshot:

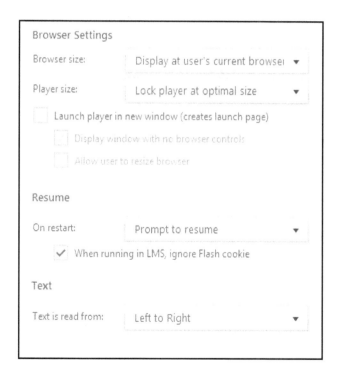

Here you can specify browser settings, resume behavior, and how you want text to be read within your player.

From the **Browser size** drop-down menu, you have the following three options:

- **Display at user's current browser size**: This is the default and will display the Story at the current size of the user's browser
- **Resize browser to optimal size**: If selected, the user's browser will automatically resize to correspond with the Story's optimal size
- **Resize browser to fill screen**: If selected, this will automatically resize the user's browser to fill the screen

From the **Player size** drop-down menu, you have the following two options:

- **Lock player at optimal size**: This is the default and will lock the player at the optimal size, even if the user resizes their browser window
- **Scale player to fill browser window**: If selected, this will scale the player to fill the user's browser window.

If you want your Story to launch in a new window, you can select **Launch player in new window**. Doing this will create a launch page. If selected, you can also define whether you want the display window containing your Story to display without browser controls (for example, print, address bar, and so on) or whether you want the user to be able to resize the browser.

Next comes the **Resume** feature. Here, you can customize how you want your Story to behave when the learner closes out the Story and then comes back to it later.

The default resume behavior is **On restart: Prompt to resume**. Personally, I am not a fan of this option and I usually change it in the resume behavior to **Never resume**. You have the following three options:

- **Prompt to resume**: If the user has previously viewed more than one slide of the Story, the user will get a message when they return to the Story asking if they would like to resume where they left off. If the user selects **Yes**, the Story will resume where they left off; if the user selects **No**, the Story will load at the beginning.
- **Always resume**: If the user reopens the Story, they will automatically be taken to the slide where they left off.
- **Never resume**: If selected, the Story will always start at the beginning.

The when running in LMS, ignore Flash cookie checkbox only applies if you choose **Prompt to resume** or **Always resume** and you are uploading your Story to an LMS. If this applies to your Story, here is how to know whether or not you need to check or uncheck the box:

- If your LMS supports bookmarking, check the box
- If your LMS does not support bookmarking, uncheck the box

Finally, Storyline allows you to enable right-to-left language support; so if you're developing a Story for a right-to-left language, you can choose **Right to Left** from the **Text is read from** drop-down menu.

Publishing your Story

Publishing your Story is important because how else will you share it with the world?! Or maybe just your target audience. You've spent all this time creating an incredible Story and now you need to publish it so that your users can experience it.

The great thing about publishing in Storyline is that you've got options! Storyline allows you to publish to the Web, Articulate Online, LMS, CD, and Microsoft Word. However, with options come decisions, so in the following pages, the hope is to help you identify which publishing option is for you and your project.

As a reminder, you can access the **Publish** panel by selecting **Publish** from the **HOME** tab (it's also available from all the tabs).

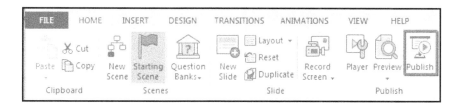

Choosing the best publishing option

When publishing a Story, you have the following five options to choose from in the Publish panel:

- **Web**: Publishing to the Web provides users access to your Story by way of the Internet/Intranet.

- If you need to track user progress, this option is not for you.

- **Articulate Online**: Publishing to Articulate Online allows you to publish your Story to Articulate's hosted LMS.
- **LMS**: Publishing to LMS provides a package that you can upload to your LMS to track user progress.
- **CD**: Publishing to CD allows you to share your Story for local use.
- **Word**: Publishing to Microsoft Word is a great way of creating a visual representation, in Microsoft Word, of your Story. This publish option comes in handy during review cycles.

Each of the publishing options will be explained and will be preceded by what occurs once you select the Publish button, which is the same for all options, with the exception of Publishing to Articulate Online or to Word.

Publishing to the Web

Publishing to the Web is the default option when you open the **Publish** panel.

Here's an explanation of each field:

- **Title**: This is the title of the Story as you want it to display in the published output.
- **...**: The **...** button beside the **Title** launches a **Project Info** panel. Populate this panel for users who will be accessing the Story using the Articulate Mobile Player.
    - **Title**: This is the title of the Story as you want it to display in the published output.
    - Thumbnail: This defaults to the first slide in the Story; however, you can change this to whichever slide you want to feature as the thumbnail—you can even use an external image if you want, which will appear in the Articulate Mobile Player library.
    - **Description**: This provides a description of the Story for users.
    - **Author, Email, Website, Duration, Date and Version**: All of the content in these fields will appear on the content information card in the Articulate Mobile player library.
    - **Identifier**: This is automatically generated and only applies to content published for LMS.
- **Description**: This provides a description of the Story for users. Currently, this is only available in the Articulate Mobile Player App; however, it is good housekeeping to include a description here.
- **Folder**: This is the destination folder for the published output. The default is `My Articulate Projects`, which was created (usually in `My Documents`) while installing the software.
- **Publishing for HTML5 and mobile devices**:
    - By default, the following are selected; deselect options as necessary:
        - **Include HTML5 Output**: This allows your Story to be viewed as HTML5 content
        - **Use Articulate Mobile Player for iOS or Android**: This optimizes your Story for use on iOS and Android devices using the Articulate Mobile Player App
        - **Allow downloading for offline viewing**: This allows users to download your Story to the Articulate Mobile Player library, where it can be viewed locally (on the downloaded device) at any time

- **Properties**:
  - **Player**: This brings up the **Player Properties** panel for any last-minute changes to the player.
  - **Quality**: This allows you to customize compression settings for your Story. The default is **Optimized for standard delivery**; however, you can modify the quality settings, within the **Publish Quality** panel, as required.

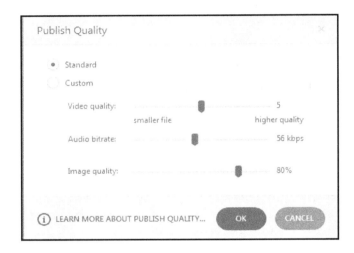

Publishing to Articulate Online

To publish to Articulate Online, select **Publish** from the **HOME** tab and then select **Articulate Online** in the **Publish** panel.

All fields are the same as previously discussed in *Publishing to the Web*, with the exception of the highlighted fields in the following screenshot:

- **Tracking**: Here, you can define how Articulate Online will track and report user progress. The default is **Slides viewed**, but you can click on this to change how the Story is tracked in the **Reporting and Tracking Options** panel.

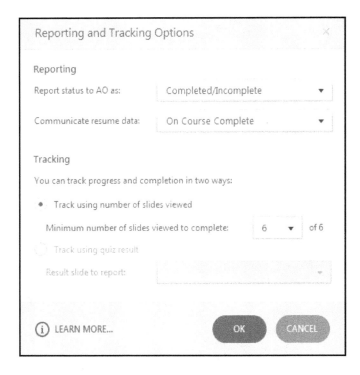

- **Report status to AO as**: From the drop-down menu, you can choose how user status is reported to Articulate Online. The options are **Completed/Incomplete**, **Passed/Incomplete**, **Passed/Failed**, and **Completed/Failed**.
- **Communicate resume data**: From the drop-down menu, you can choose how Articulate Online reports resume data. The options are **On Course Complete** and **After Every Slide**.
- **Tracking**: Here you can select whether you want to track user progress by number of slides viewed, and if so, you can specify the minimum number of slides viewed to consider the Story complete. Or, you can track user progress using a quiz result, and if so, you will need to specify the result slide to report.
- **Account Information**: Here you need to enter your Articulate Online login credentials.
    - Please note that there is a manual upload option available, but you will need to define this ahead of time in **Storyline Options** within the **File** menu.

Once you click on **PUBLISH**, your content will be published and uploaded to Articulate

Online. Once the **Publish Successful** panel appears, you can select **Manage Content** to access the published output on Articulate Online, where you can then manage the content.

Publishing to LMS

To publish to LMS, select **Publish** from the **HOME** tab and then select LMS on the **Publish** panel.

All fields are the same as previously discussed in *Publishing to the Web* and in **Publishing to Articulate Online**, with a couple of exceptions:

- The Tracking functionality is more robust in terms of customization when publishing to LMS.
- There are **Output Options**:

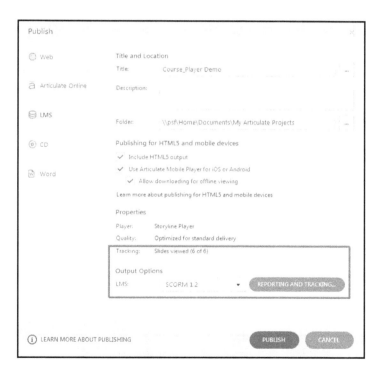

- **Tracking**: The default is **Slides viewed**; however, if you select **Slides viewed**, the **Reporting and Tracking Options** panel will appear, where you have additional options. There is a button leading to this panel in the **Output Options**, so we'll talk about the additional options in a moment.

- **Output Options**: Here, you will want to specify the type of output you want; this typically depends on what type of output a given LMS can support, so you'll want to find out which output is appropriate for your LMS:

  - **LMS**: There are four options, **SCORM 1.2**, **SCORM 2004**, **AICC**, and **Tin Can API**.
  - **REPORTING AND TRACKING...**: Selecting this button will bring up the **Reporting and Tracking Options** panel. This is where you will define how your LMS tracks and reports user progress:

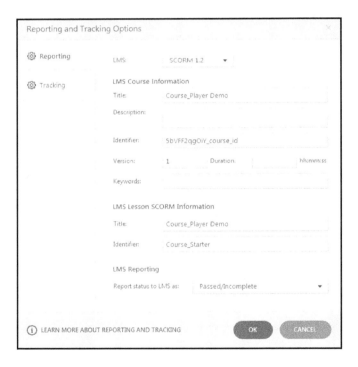

- Based on your previous LMS output selection, the **Reporting** tab will be largely populated automatically. However, you can certainly enter in a course **Description** or **Keywords** if it has not yet been populated. The important part here will be the final section of the **Reporting** tab.

- **Report status to LMS as**: Here, as with *Publishing to Articulate Online*, you will need to specify how you want the user status to be reported to the LMS.
- The **Tracking** tab is where you will define how user progress is tracked, the minimum number of slides for completion, or the results slide you want the LMS to report.
    - Please note that if you choose a number of slides less than the total number of slides, you are unable to specify the slides to be viewed.

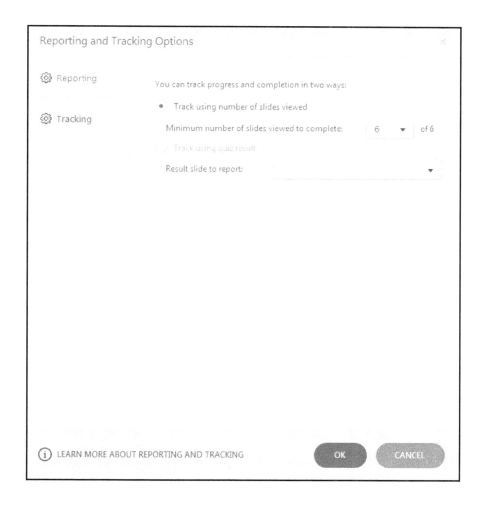

Publishing to CD

To publish to CD, select **Publish** from the **HOME** tab and then select CD in the **Publish** panel.

All fields are the same as previously discussed in *Publishing to the Web*; however, there aren't as many fields and/or options.

Publishing to Word

Publishing to Word is so helpful during review cycles! To publish to Word, select **Publish** from the **HOME** tab and then select Word on the **Publish** panel.

As with all previously discussed publish options, the **Title**, **Project Info**, **Description**, and

Folder fields are the same. However, publishing to word has an added **Properties** section.

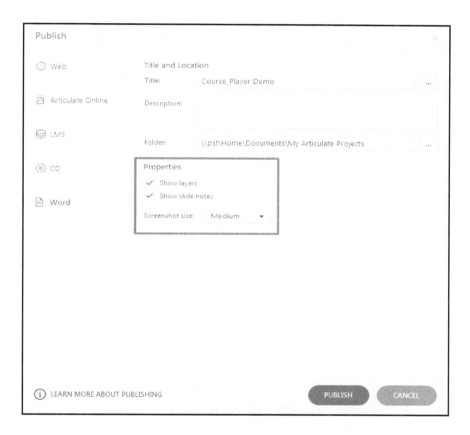

- **Show layers**: Selecting this will show content from slide layers; without this selected, you will only see base layer content in the published output.
- **Show slide notes**: Selecting this will show both the onscreen content and the slide notes. This is especially handy when your **Notes** panel contains more information than your onscreen content, or if your **Notes** panel is acting as a course transcript.
- **Screenshot size**: Here, you will select whether you want a medium or large-size screenshot of each slide to be included in the published output.

Publishing

When you've selected your publishing options and you're ready to publish, regardless of which option you chose, your Story will go through the publishing process, and once complete, you will be presented with additional options.

When publishing to the Web, you will have the following six options:

- **VIEW PROJECT**: This allows you to launch and view your published output
- **EMAIL**: If selected, this option will open a new e-mail with a zipped file of your published output included as an attachment
- **FTP**: If selected, this option will open a panel to enter your FTP credentials, allowing you to transfer your published output to a website
- **ZIP**: This option creates a zipped file containing your published output, which comes in handy if you plan to upload to Articulate Tempshare or an LMS
- **OPEN**: This opens the folder containing your published output
- **HTML5**: This opens the HTML5 version of your published output in your default web browser

When publishing to LMS, CD, or Word, you will have all of the options available when publishing to the Web, except HTML5.

- Additionally, when publishing to Word, the **VIEW PROJECT** button changes to read **VIEW DOCUMENT**, which, when selected, will open the published Word document in Microsoft Word.

Publishing to Dropbox or Google Drive

To publish and upload your Storyline output using `https://www.dropbox.com/`, follow these steps:

1. Download and install the Dropbox app.
2. Drag your `output` folder to your `Dropbox`.
3. Open `Dropbox` and drag the `output` folder to the `Public` folder.
4. Open the uploaded folder within the `Public` folder and right-click on the `story.html` file.
5. Select **Copy Public Link**.
6. Open a new browser tab, paste the copied link and press *Enter*.

If these instructions confuse you, I created a handy screencast that explains both processes; you can access that video at `https://vimeo.com/108414673`.

Summary

This chapter showed you just how easily you can modify the default Storyline course player to create a customized experience for your clients and users. With all of the built-in functionality Storyline provides, your customization is really only limited by your own creativity.

Publishing your Story is a critical milestone because without publishing, your audience will never get to experience your stories! Storyline provides you with multiple options to publish your stories in whichever output format you require. In addition to publishing, this chapter shared several methods of uploading and sharing your Storyline output so that you can get stories to your users as efficiently as possible.

In the next chapter, your mind will be filled with tons of ideas for harnessing your inner creativity to do some really neat things in Storyline, based on what you've learned throughout the previous chapters.

8

Becoming More Creative

Now that you've learned how to take your Storyline skills up a notch by creating cool menu effects, leveraging the capabilities of motion path animations, variables, and JavaScript, you might feel mentally exhausted, or you might feel like a Storyline whiz and are wondering what's next. You've learned all of these new things, but now your brain is tapping out when it comes to creativity. Don't worry. This chapter has got you covered!

The purpose of this chapter is to give you some ideas to really flex your creativity muscles. We'll talk about what you can do to challenge yourself, how you can harness your inner creativity, including where to locate free assets, and where you can learn more about Articulate Storyline.

This chapter will focus on providing loads of examples to help fill your creativity bank with tons of ideas. The hope is that by the end of this chapter your brain will be overflowing with ideas for creating your next greatest story!

In this chapter, we will discuss the following topics:

- Challenging yourself
- Harness your inner creativity
- Keep learning!

Challenge yourself

Challenging yourself is exactly how it sounds—a challenge! Sometimes you're feeling tapped out for ideas, and when your boss or client asks you to come up with a custom Storyline template, you may feel like bashing your head on your keyboard due to lack of creativity… but there are always options!

You need to make something your muse and run with it, so the goal of the next section is to provide you with ideas to challenge your creativity.

Create your own assets

One way of challenging yourself is to create your own assets. This could be learning how to take your own stock photographs, building out vector-based imagery in PowerPoint or Storyline using the shapes and grouping functions, or creating your own videos, just to name a few.

The benefit of creating your own assets is that they're yours! You can use them however you see fit, you can share them with communities, you can easily modify them, and you can include them in your portfolio. If you're feeling extra entrepreneurial, you can create a repository of themes or downloads and sell them for a profit.

Within Storyline, you can easily create your own assets using shapes. You just need to be a little creative. To create assets using shapes, you just need to break the object you wish to create down into the most basic of shapes.

For example, if you wanted to create a corkboard with a note, you might want to follow these steps:

1. First, select the rectangle shape and create a large rectangle on your slide. This will become your corkboard.
2. Right-click on the rectangle and select **Format Shape**. Then, under fill, choose **Picture** or **Texture fill**, and from the **Texture** drop-down menu, choose an appropriate texture and then click on **Close**.
3. With the rectangle still selected, choose **Shape Outline** from the **Format** tab, select **Weight**, and choose 8px. This will create a thicker outline, mimicking the border material typically seen around a corkboard.
4. For the note, use the rectangle shape to create a rectangle or square. From **Shape Fill** on the **Format** tab, choose an appropriate color for the note. From **Shape Outline**, select **No Outline**.
5. Place the note shape on the corkboard, and using the **Rotation** option, you can change the rotation if you want.
6. Next, you will want to create a tack. To do so, use the circle shape to create a small circle. Change the **Shape Fill** color to an appropriate color, then, for added realism, choose **Shape Effects** | **Shadow** and add a shadow to the shape.
7. Finally, position the tack over the note shape so that it looks as though the circle shape is holding the rectangle shape to the corkboard. Your asset should look

similar to the following screenshot:

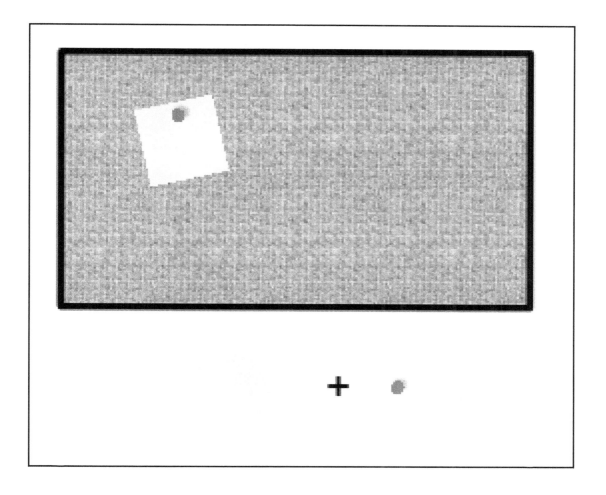

 You can take your assets one step further and group them as one object. Once you have all of your assets combined, select them all and press *Ctrl + G*.

You can use these same principles to create many different media assets! A very practical way of using these principles is to create custom navigation. This requires a bit more finesse, in that you also have to add triggers, but the principles stay the same. For example, you can create custom previous and next buttons, similar to those shown in the following image (and styled however your story requires):

To make these shapes behave like functioning members of your story, select one as the next button and one as your previous button. Then, add a trigger with the following parameters:

- **Action**: **Jump to slide**
- **Slide**: next slide (or previous, depending on which shape you're adding a trigger to)
- **When**: **User clicks**
- **Object**: (the shape)

Then, select **Slide Properties** (1), and from the **Slide navigation controls** section, uncheck **Prev** and **Next** (2).

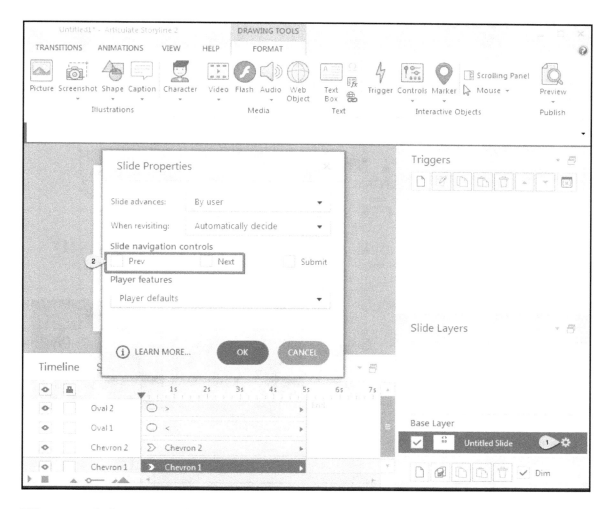

When you click on **OK** and preview your slide, you will notice that the default **Prev** and **Next** buttons have been removed, and your custom navigation is now controlling advancement for your story.

When using custom navigation, you will need to copy the navigation and paste it to each slide, or add it to the slide master, to ensure that it is applied to all slides in your story.

Web resources

`Pinterest.com` is a fantastic resource for all things, not just design, but whenever feeling defeated, I hop on over to Pinterest and go down a wormhole of search terms, often looking at design elements. These elements ideas can be pulled from branding, or web design, or magazines.

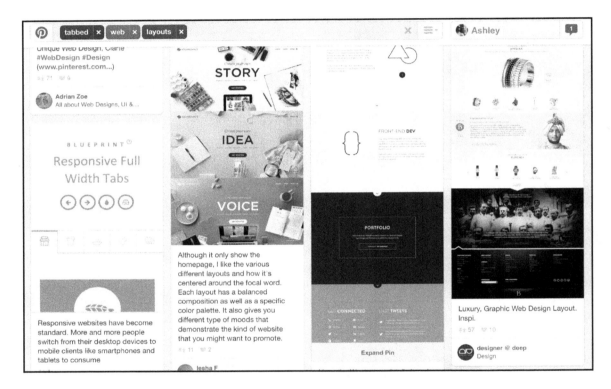

Another way to get your creative juices flowing is to take a look at color palettes. Coming up with a color palette for your story can be a jumping off point that sends you into warp speed when it comes to development.

`ColourLovers.com` is a fantastic resource for color palettes and patterns. As a creative community, members share color palettes and patterns, and you can easily search for appropriate palettes for any project!

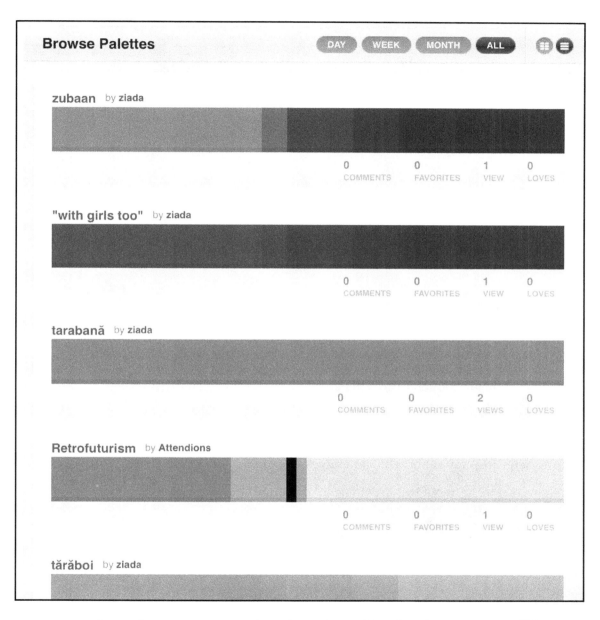

`Coolors.co` is another great resource for color palettes. Entering the generator will let you peruse color palettes with ease by simply pressing the spacebar until you reach a palette that works for you.

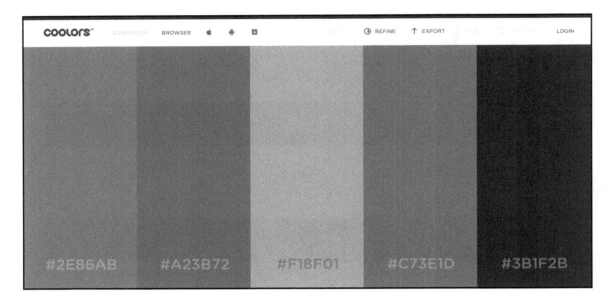

The Articulate E-Learning Heroes Community (`https://community.articulate.com/`) is a seemingly never-ending resource for design ideas. Whether you're looking for inspiration for media assets, tips and tricks, or templates, the E-Learning Heroes Community is a one-stop shop. Even if you're struggling to find what you're looking for, a quick post in the discussion form will likely yield a quick onslaught of responses from community members.

Search the community with ease and check out all of the articles and free downloads for a taste of e-learning inspiration! Sometimes being able to see what your colleagues are doing can be a huge inspiration for what you might want to develop in the future.

Another great thing about the Articulate E-Learning Heroes Community is that David Anderson, the Articulate Community Manager, posts weekly e-learning challenges, and these weekly challenges have been instrumental in e-learning portfolio building for many community members. If you're struggling with a creativity block, these weekly challenges can really help you over that bump.

Harness your inner creativity

You are creative and you can easily harness your inner creativity, but half of the battle is finding design inspiration. Hopefully, the aforementioned resources will help get your creative juices flowing. However, there are a few more ideas that we'll discuss in the next section.

Modifying existing assets

Circling back to the Articulate E-Learning Heroes Community, within this community is a handy downloads section. Within this downloads section, there are community member-provided free downloads for many existing assets, from templates, to course assets, to course design resources.

You can access the Articulate E-Learning Heroes Community Downloads section at `https://community.articulate.com/downloads`.

This resource is essential for any e-learning developer, but another great thing is that because these resources have been made freely available for download, you can download any of the assets and use them as is, or modify them to suit the needs of your project. Alternatively, you can use them as a jumping off point when it comes to design inspiration!

 Attribution is always nice, if it's possible. Just because it's free doesn't mean that someone didn't spend their own time developing the asset!

Using free resources

In addition to the free resources found in the Articulate E-Learning Heroes Community downloads section, the Internet has an unending pool of potential resources just kicking around!

Creative Market

`Creativemarket.com` is a paid resource that offers several free resources each Monday. Often these are vector-based graphics, and these assets can easily be manipulated in Adobe Illustrator. Creative Market free downloads are also a great way of building a unique font collection, so keep checking back each week!

When it comes to the paid side of things, Creative Market offers a broad range of downloads (for example, graphics, templates, documents, photographs, and so on), with very affordable licensing prices. Additionally, Creative Market also has specials where you can download hundreds of assets in a bundle for a set, reasonable purchase price.

The weekly free goods can be accessed at `https://creativemarket.com/free-goods`, so add that link to your favorites!

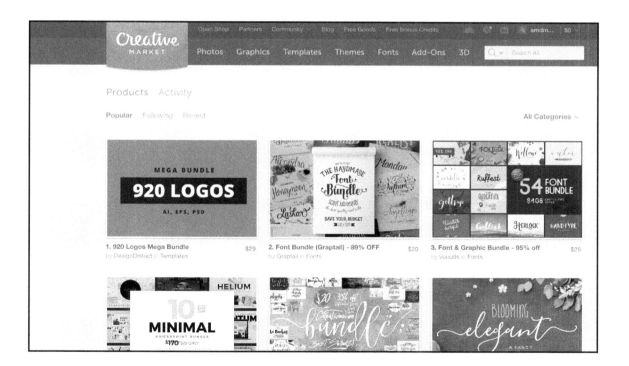

Unsplash

`Unsplash.com` is a go-to resource for finding free stock photos. It's often the first place I think to go when looking for professional-quality background images. This is also a great resource for finding design inspiration, as scrolling through photo upon photo can really get the creative juices flowing!

 To access the glory that is Unsplash, refer to `http://unsplash.com`.

The Noun Project

The Noun Project is a user-submitted icon repository, which can be extremely handy when it comes to e-learning development as you can locate almost any icon you can think of to search for.

You can download icons for free, with attribution, or you can purchase icons for a very reasonable cost to use royalty free.

To access The Noun Project, refer to `https://thenounproject.com/`.

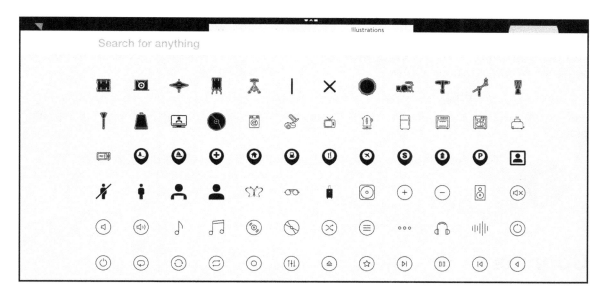

These are only a few free resources available, but hopefully it's enough to get your creative juices flowing!

Keep learning!

When working in learning development, regardless of your role, you should never stop learning! Technology is always changing and evolving, and it's important that us learning professionals stay on top of the latest and greatest developments.

Luckily, there are a lot of great opportunities to keep learning, and the following are some recommendations.

Articulate E-Learning Heroes Community

As I've mentioned several times in this chapter alone, the Articulate E-Learning Heroes Community truly is a fountain of knowledge. The tutorials section covers just about anything you'd ever want to know about Articulate Storyline or Articulate Studio.

 To access the Storyline tutorials, refer to `https://community.articulate.com/hubs/storyline`, and to access the Studio tutorials, refer to `https://community.articulate.com/hubs/articulate-studio`.

For anything else your mind is itching to find out, just post a question in the forum and another E-Learning Heroes Community member is likely to respond expediently. If not, someone from Articulate will!

Again, the weekly E-Learning Heroes challenges are a great place to learn because you'll learn from tangible examples provided by members in the community—it really is a great place.

 To access all of the Articulate E-Learning Heroes Challenges, refer to `https://community.articulate.com/series/e-learning-challenges`.

Courses

Instructional Design Essentials: Models of ID by Shea Hanson:
`http://www.lynda.com/Higher-Education-tutorials/Instructional-Design-Essentials-Models-ID/161318-2.html`

Up and Running With Articulate Storyline 2 by David Rivers:
`http://www.lynda.com/Storyline-tutorials/Up-Running-Articulate-Storyline-2/196582-2.html?srchtrk=index%3a1%0alinktypeid%3a2%0aq%3astoryline%0apage%3a1%0as%3arelevance%0asa%3atrue%0aproducttypeid%3a2`

Articulate Storyline Advanced Techniques by Daniel Brigham:
`http://www.lynda.com/Storyline-tutorials/Articulate-Storyline-Advanced-Techniques/145209-2.html?srchtrk=index%3a1%0alinktypeid%3a2%0aq%3astoryline%0apage%3a1%0as%3arelevance%0asa%3atrue%0aproducttypeid%3a2`

Articulate Storyline 2 by Inception Labs:
`https://www.udemy.com/articulate-storyline2/`

Books

This is in no way an exclusive list of books, but these are my top resource books when it comes to learning and development.

Articulate Storyline Essentials by Ashley Chiasson:
`https://www.packtpub.com/hardware-and-creative/articulate-storyline-essentials`

Learning Articulate Storyline by Stephanie Harnett:
`https://www.packtpub.com/hardware-and-creative/learning-articulate-storyline`

Design for How People Learn by Julie Dirksen:
`http://www.amazon.com/Design-People-Learn-Voices-Matter/dp/0134211286/ref=sr_1_1?ie=UTF8&qid=1460037333&sr=8-1&keywords=design+for+how+people+learn`

Show Your Work by Jane Bozarth:
`http://www.amazon.com/Show-Your-Work-Jane-Bozarth/dp/1118863623/ref=sr_1_3?ie=UTF8&qid=1460037359&sr=8-3&keywords=show+your+work`

How We Learn: The Surprising Truth About When, Where, and Why it Happens by Benedict
Carey: `http://www.amazon.com/How-We-Learn-Surprising-Happens/dp/0812984293/ref=sr_1_1?ie=UTF8&qid=1460037378&sr=8-1&keywords=benedict+carey`

Slide:ology: The Art and Science of Creating Great Presentations by Nancy Duarte:
`http://www.amazon.com/slide-ology-Science-Creating-Presentations/dp/0596522347/ref=sr_1_3?ie=UTF8&qid=1460037411&sr=8-3&keywords=nancy+durante`

Resonate: Present Visual Stories that Transform Audiences by Nancy Duarte:
`http://www.amazon.com/Resonate-Present-Stories-Transform-Audiences/dp/0470632011/ref=sr_1_1?ie=UTF8&qid=1460037411&sr=8-1&keywords=nancy+durante`

Illuminate: Ignite Change through Speeches, Stories, Ceremonies, and Symbols by Nancy Duarte and Patti
Sanchez: `http://www.amazon.com/Illuminate-Through-Speeches-Stories-Ceremonies/dp/1101980168/ref=sr_1_2?ie=UTF8&qid=1460037411&sr=8-2&keywords=nancy+durante`

The Gamification of Learning and Instruction Fieldbook: Ideas into Practice by Karl M. Kapp, Lucas Blair, and Rich

Mesch: `http://www.amazon.com/Gamification-Learning-Instruction-Fieldbook-Practice/dp/111867443X/ref=sr_1_2?ie=UTF8&qid=1460037508&sr=8-2&keywords=karl+kapp`

Summary

In this chapter, you were provided with all of the resources I can think of to get you moving along with igniting your creative spark and beginning your journey down the path to phenomenal e-learning development.

Throughout this book, you've navigated from the more basic concepts to the more advanced concepts and should now be able to comfortably leverage the full potential of Articulate Storyline. We've covered a lot of ground, so please read and reread sections as necessary, explore all of the exercise files, and go forth and conquer all of your e-learning dreams!

It's almost time for me to say goodbye, but before I do, I'll leave you with an appendix that provides helpful tips for streamlining your Storyline development.

Appendix
Streamlining Your Development

The goal of this appendix is to provide you with additional information related to methods for streamlining your development within Articulate Storyline. You may be a Storyline master, but there is always room for optimization and efficiency.

By providing tips and recommendations, I am confident you will be able to develop your e-learning in the most efficient manner possible!

There are never enough hours in the day, but with all of the functionality Storyline provides, there certainly are options for streamlining your development. Maybe your way of doing things took three steps, but only needs to take one or two. However you develop, the goal here is to help you turn your development into a well-oiled machine, removing redundancy wherever we can!

In the following chapter, we will discuss a handful of simple ways for making Storyline work for you and your purposes. If you implement even half of these suggestions, your development should become speedier, even if it's just by a hair. Becoming more efficient can potentially correlate to reducing your work hours or being able to take on additional projects, so use these tips to your advantage!

Using a style guide

Style guides are typically client-generated. However, you can create your own if you think it will streamline your Storyline development. This can be especially important in team situations where multiple developers will be working on one project.

Style guides are documented explanations and illustrations of stylistic options available for the products in development. These stylistic options typically include approved logos and branding, colors (and corresponding hex values), appropriate fonts and sizes, and can even be so specific as to dictate the pixel width of a highlight box or the screen resolution the product must adhere to.

Basically, the style guide indicates how your story should look or feel and attempts to stay on *brand*, based on project specifications. Other elements may even include the tone of voice used or grammar preferences.

Using a style guide during your Storyline development can help streamline your development approach in terms of reducing rework. When your story comes back from review, if you've used a style guide, you will likely have fewer stylistic comments to address and most of the comments will be related to content and/or functionality.

Style guides also ensure consistency across stories, so if multiple developers are working on the same project, they should all look and feel similar to one another if the developer adhered to specifications within the style guide.

Setting up autorecovery

Storyline 2 has an autorecovery feature, which can really save your butt when you're deep in the trenches of development and your software or computer crashes.

To set up this feature, you will need to save your new project at least once so that Storyline has something to autorecover from. Then, select **File | Storyline Options**. Here, you will see **Save AutoRecovery information every _ minutes**. Define how often you want to save autorecovery and click on **OK**.

While Storyline has the aforementioned autorecovery functionality, there are some broader concepts that you should be aware of when it comes to avoiding the loss of your Storyline content, including, but not limited to:

- Do not save to external drives: Saving locally is your best bet to ensure nothing happens to your Storyline file. What does this mean? Save to your local drive. Saving to external storage devices may result in freezing or file corruption.
- Save regularly: Saving regularly can prevent a lot of heartache and human resources. In Storyline, whenever you see an asterisk in the project title (as shown in the following screenshot), this indicates that changes have been made. Don't rely on autorecovery, just hit *Ctrl + S*; it's quick and easy!

```
Course_Starter.story* - Articulate Storyline 2
```

- Version your stories! Versioning is a best practice for any project, in any authoring tool, but it can definitely save you some effort if another version becomes corrupt. If you maintain multiple versions of your projects, you can always revert back to a previous version if necessary. It's very similar to the backups that Windows and Mac OS create of your hard drives. When it comes to versioning, the best advice would be to version whenever you are addressing review comments and whenever there have been significant changes made to your files.
- Maintain a backup (or multiple backups): I'm of the mind that the more backups you maintain, the better. It may seem like overkill, but if one backup method fails, the others can pick up the slack and save your butt! For backups, the following are my preferences:
  - Local backups: Locally, it's good to maintain at least one backup, especially for projects that require a lot of effort or are quite large
  - External backups: For external backups, I maintain one backup on a wired external drive, and the second backup I maintain is through an automated backup using Time Capsule for Mac

You can check out the two backups I prefer at
http://www.apple.com/shop/product/ME182LL/A/airport-time-capsule-3tb?fnode=5f and
http://www.amazon.com/Black-Passport-Ultra-Portable-External/dp/B00W8XXYN2/ref=sr_1_4?s=pc&ie=UTF8&qid=1460114855&sr=1-4&keywords=wd+external+hard+drive.

  - Online storage: Maintain project backups in the cloud using services such as Google Drive or Dropbox (or both, if you're really cautious)

Using hot keys

Hot keys are keyboard shortcuts, which are software-specific. Once you memorize a software's hot keys, you can easily improve your efficiency. When it comes to Storyline, you have many options for streamlining your development with the following hot keys:

Function	Hot Keys
Copy	*Ctrl + C*
Duplicate	*Ctrl + D*
Cut	*Ctrl + X*
Paste	*Ctrl + V*
Undo	*Ctrl + Z*
Redo	*Ctrl + Y*
Select All	*Ctrl + A*
Add Slide	*Ctrl + M*
Add Text Box	*Ctrl + T*
Add Image	*Ctrl + J*
Add Hyperlink	*Ctrl + K*
Move Object 1 Pixel	*Ctrl* + Arrow (in desired direction)
Move or Resize	*Ctrl* + Drag (moves/resizes in 1 pixel increments)
Move to Straight Line	*Shift* + Drag
Group Objects	*Ctrl + G*
Ungroup Objects	*Ctrl + Shift + G*
Copy Formatting	*Ctrl + Shift + C*
Paste Formatting	*Ctrl + Shift + V*
Format Shape	*Ctrl + Enter*
Add Cue Point	*C*

Pause/Play When Using Timeline Play Controls	Spacebar
Bold Font	*Ctrl + B*
Italic Font	*Ctrl + I*
Underline Font	*Ctrl + U*
Left Align Text	*Ctrl + L*
Center Align Text	*Ctrl + E*
Right Align Text	*Ctrl + R*
Find	*Ctrl + F*
Spell Check	*F7*
Select All Text Within Selected Object	*F2*
Preview Current Slide	*Ctrl + F12*
Preview Current Scene	*Shift + F12*
Preview Project	*F12*
Normal View	*F3*
Slide Master	*F4*
Feedback Master	*F5*
Publish Project	*F10*
Show/Hide Gridlines	*Shift + F9*
Zoom In or Out	*Ctrl* + Mouse Wheel
Open Project	*Ctrl + O*
Save Project	*Ctrl + S*
Close Tab	*Ctrl + W*

Mike Taylor, a former Articulate Community Manager, developed a keyboard shortcut job aid for Storyline. You can access it at `https://community.articulate.com/download/storyline-keyboard-shortcuts`.

Using the Quick Access Toolbar

If using keyboard shortcuts is not so much your style, Storyline gives you another option for making your e-learning development process a well-oiled machine: the Quick Access Toolbar!

The Quick Access Toolbar is an area along the top of your screen that's reserved for adding shortcuts to commonly used elements in Storyline. This toolbar is complete customizable and can house any shortcut you want.

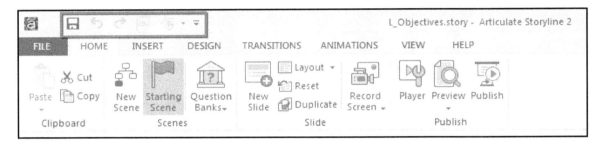

Adding icons to the Quick Access Toolbar is easy. All you have to do is right-click the element you wish to add to the tool bar and select **Add to Quick Access Toolbar**.

To delete something from the Quick Access Toolbar, simply right-click on the icon and select **Remove from Quick Access Toolbar**.

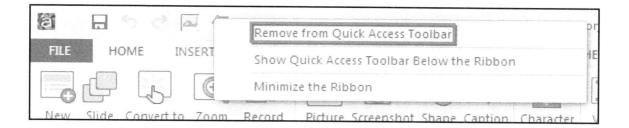

Using the Format Painter

As in many Microsoft products, the Format Painter in Articulate Storyline allows you to copy the formatting of one object and apply it to another object, be it text, button styling, and so on. This feature is a huge time-saver when it comes to development.

To use the Format Painter, select the object you want to copy formatting from (**1**), then select the **Format Painter** icon from the **HOME** tab (**2**), and then select the object you want to copy the formatting to (**3**).

If you double-click on the Format Painter, you can apply formatting to multiple objects.

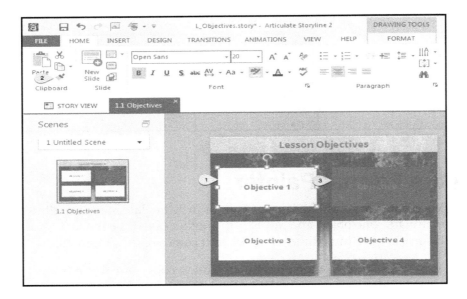

You will notice that the formatting has changed accordingly for the receiving object.

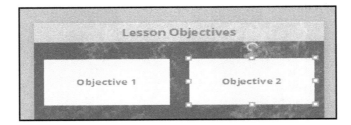

The Format Painter also applies to formatting states. If you want to apply a consistent format to states of multiple objects, or of one object, then select the formatted object, choose the Format Painter, and select the object you wish to apply the formatting to. When you look at the **States** panel, you will notice the same states have been applied.

Storyline 2 took the Format Painter one step further by providing an Animation Painter. With this tool, you can copy the animation from one object and apply it to another object without having to manually do so.

To do so, first select the object you wish to copy the animation from (**1**), then select **Animation Painter** from the **ANIMATIONS** tab (**2**), and then select the object you wish to copy the animation to (**3**).

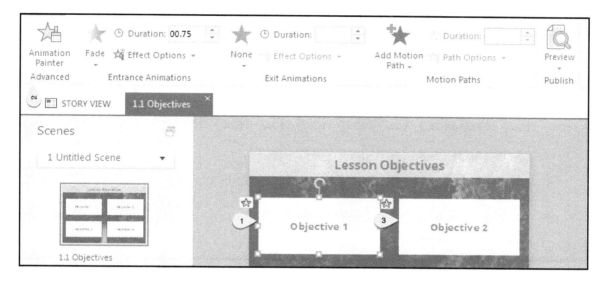

You will notice that the copied animation has been applied to the selected object.

Using cue points

When you're working with audio, video, or even with multiple objects on a slide, cue points can be particularly useful in reducing the amount of time you spend laboring over synchronization.

Cue points indicate when you want something to happen or when you want to cue something to happen.

In the following screenshot, we're looking at the timeline for a slide. On this particular slide, we have some audio and four objects. The objects have been staggered to indicate they are to appear one after another, but if you want to align them to the audio, cue points can help with that.

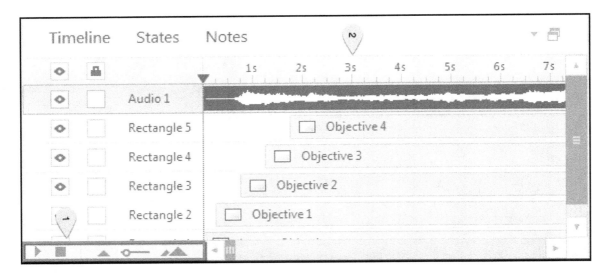

Using the play controls (**1**), you can play the audio track, and whenever you want an object to appear, simply press C. This will create a cue point on the timeline (**2**).

Once you've added your cue points, you can right-click on each object on the timeline you wish to align and select which cue point you wish to align the object to. The object will then snap to that area on the timeline.

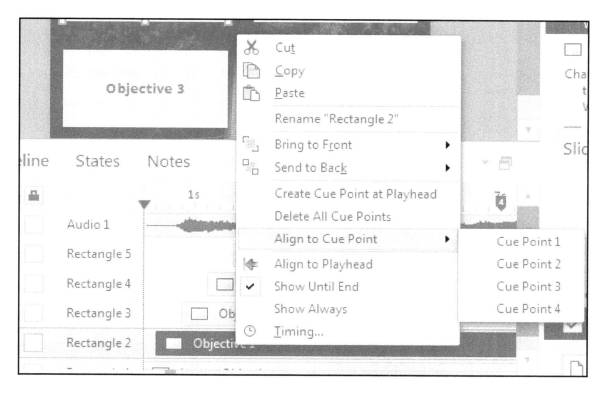

Once you have cue points on your timeline, you can move them around, delete individual cue points by right-clicking on the cue point and selecting **Delete Cue Point**, or delete all cue points from the timeline by right-clicking on a cue point and selecting **Delete All Cue Points**.

If you have a project heavy in text/audio synchronization, you will quickly realize how much of a time-saving miracle cue points in Articulate Storyline are. You can also use cue points in tandem with **When**: **Timeline Reaches trigger**, triggering an action to occur when the timeline reaches a specified cue point.

Using Slide Masters

Slide Masters can greatly streamline your development, in that they allow you to predevelop all of your screen styles and then pull from them, like a bank of screen styles, for use in your development. They take a bit of effort upfront, but the payoff is huge, especially when it comes to large projects. Slide Masters can also be extremely effective at ensuring a consistent look and feel, particularly on projects that have multiple developers.

In Chapter 7, *Assessing Learners*, we talked about Feedback Masters. Slide Masters work in the same manner as Feedback Masters, except they apply to all of the content slides. To avoid redundancy, review this content and apply it to the concept of Slide Masters. These also work similar to the Slide Masters used in Microsoft Office products.

To access and manage the Slide Master in Storyline, select **SLIDE MASTER** from the **VIEW** tab, as shown in the following screenshot. Your Slide Master will open; here, you can modify your Slide Masters.

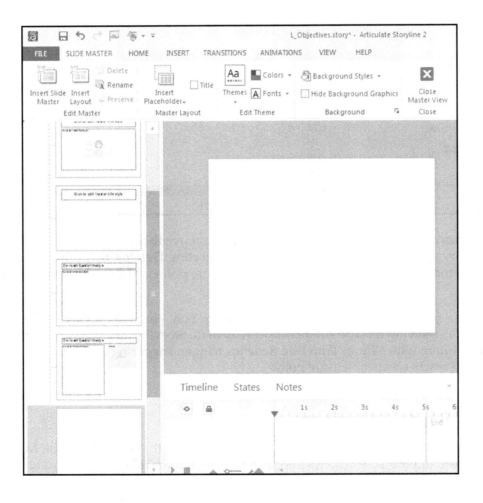

Translating content

Storyline makes translation easy! All you have to do is choose **File | Translation | Export**. This will allow you to export your project as a Microsoft Word document. You can keep the default project name or rename the file accordingly.

Once exported, the document can be translated. You have to do this or farm out the task of translation. Storyline is good, but it can only do so much. Once translated, simply select **File | Translation | Import**, choose the appropriate file, and your translation will import into Storyline.

 When you're ready to import, remember to save the Story file with a suffix such as _FRENCH to ensure you're not overwriting your original file—that would suck.

Staying up to date

This may seem like an odd recommendation when it comes to streamlining your development, but it's really not. The folks at Articulate are always making product improvements and updates to their software. You can always check for new software updates in Storyline by selecting **Check for Updates** from the **HELP** tab.

If updates are available, you will be presented with the **Update Available** prompt, where you can choose whether you want to view updates.

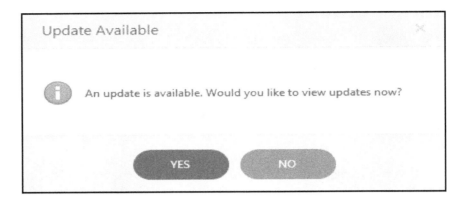

Now, the reason why staying up to date with your software plays a role in streamlining your development is that if Articulate has fixed bugs from a previous version, it can save you time searching for information as to why something in your project isn't working!

Testing

Testing your stories before submitting them to clients can save you a lot of time spent reworking development post-review. It also ensures that your clients are confident in your abilities.

Before submitting stories for review, you should ensure that you are testing the entire story, interacting with all elements on each screen, and ensuring that all slides work in the manner for which they were developed. If not, revise accordingly.

A good recommendation is to develop a test case document where you outline all of the elements you want to check during your review, as this will allow you to essentially go through a quick checklist during your review to ensure everything has been reviewed from a quality assurance standpoint. Test case checklists should be project-specific and include elements featured in the project requirements document or Statement of Work.

Another recommendation is to try and break your story each time you review it and interact with all the buttons, toggling back and forth, and forward and backward to attempt to call out any erratic behavior that your reviewers may experience. Doing this upfront will reduce any unanticipated review comments related to misbehaving functionality.

Summary

This appendix provided you with a handful of options explaining how easily you can streamline your development within Articulate Storyline. Hopefully, you now have a whole arsenal of tools necessary to go forth and conquer your e-learning goals. Good luck!

Index